# Review: 1979 Session of Congress

AEI LEGISLATIVE ANALYSES

*Balanced analyses of current proposals before the Congress, prepared with the help of specialists in law, economics, and government*

# Review: 1979 Session of the Congress

## 1979

### 96th Congress
### 1st Session

AMERICAN ENTERPRISE INSTITUTE
*for Public Policy Research*
*Washington, D.C.*

ISBN  0-8447-0228-5
Legislative Analysis No. 13, 96th Congress
January 1980

# Contents

The first session of the 96th Congress stretched late into December, as members grappled with major energy bills and legislation on federal loan guarantees for the financially beleaguered Chrysler Corporation. Summer gas lines and rumors of future gasoline and heating oil shortages focused public and congressional attention on energy issues, to the detriment of other, less politically visible legislation. Although major bills affecting U.S. foreign policy and international trade were passed by the 96th Congress, their national prominence was considerably less than might otherwise have been the case.

Energy issues dominated congressional debate during the latter half of 1979, with double-digit inflation compounding the difficulties inherent in legislating belt-tightening energy measures. Standby gas rationing and energy conservation programs, and low-income fuel assistance were passed after lengthy and sometimes bitter debate. The energy bills passed represent compromises among conflicting political, regional, and economic interests. Legislation on synthetic fuels, the windfall profits tax, and a priority energy projects program was also heatedly discussed, but no final action was taken.

In foreign affairs, the Congress passed legislation implementing provisions of the Panama Canal treaty. The diplomatic recognition of the People's Republic of China and the consequent severing of official relations with Taiwan led to passage of a bill to maintain cultural, economic, and defense ties with the island nation. Important international trade bills included legislation implementing agreements reached in the Tokyo round of the Multilateral Trade Negotiations (MTN), a bill regulating the export of advanced technology, and President Carter's trade reorganization plan. The Senate did not reach a consensus on strategic arms limitation (SALT II), and its consideration has now been delayed indefinitely.

In the domestic arena, the creation of the cabinet-level Department of Education was a major development. That legislation and the revisions in the food stamp program passed the Congress with some debate, but little hardcore opposition. Hospital cost containment was not enacted after the administration proposal was weakened substantially by the House. Efforts to control spending by political action committees and to reform the lobbying law were also shelved. Several bills on national health insurance were introduced, but the issue is expected to be more hotly contested during the 1980 session.

Legislation not passed by the 96th Congress is as noteworthy as much of the legislation that was enacted. In general, legislation dealing with economic, social, and environmental issues took a back seat to the more politically prominent energy bills. Regulatory reform efforts suffered a similar fate. The Congress was able—with some difficulty—to approve a 5.5 percent pay rise for its members and for federal employees earning over $47,500, bringing congressional salaries to $60,662.50 annually. The first session of the 96th Congress was in session for 354 days, and passed 188 bills, all but one of which were approved by the president as public laws. In comparison, 223 bills were enacted in 1977 and 410 in 1978.

MAJOR LEGISLATION—1979 SESSION

Among the most significant bills passed during the first session of the 96th Congress were:

- major energy legislation, including standby gas rationing and low-income fuel assistance (P.L. 96-102, P.L. 96-126)
- establishment of a cabinet-level Department of Education (P.L. 96-88)
- restructuring of the bankrupt Milwaukee Railroad (P.L. 96-101)
- reorganization of government agencies dealing with international trade (Reorganization Plan No. 3 of 1979)
- revision of U.S. export policy, including the export of advanced technology (P.L. 96-72)
- legislation implementing results of the Tokyo round of the Multilateral Trade Negotiations (P.L. 96-39)
- legislation defining U.S. rights and responsibilities in the Panama Canal Zone (P.L. 96-70)
- provision for nongovernmental relations with Taiwan after the diplomatic recognition of the People's Republic of China (P.L. 96-8)
- revision of appropriations for, and monitoring and information requirements of, the food stamp program (P.L. 96-58)
- legislation guaranteeing loans to the Chrysler Corporation (P.L. 96-185)
- restructuring of the Law Enforcement Assistance Administration, including creation of three new support agencies within the Justice Department (P.L. 96-157).

Other important legislation passed during 1979 included:

- Amtrak reorganization (P.L. 96-73)
- pipeline safety requirements for natural gas (P.L. 96-129)
- removal of restrictions on foreign aid to Uganda (P.L. 96-67)
- authorization to complete Tellico Dam (P.L. 96-69)
- congressional and federal executive pay raises (P.L. 96-86)
- refugee assistance and Caribbean hurricane relief assistance (P.L. 96-110, P.L. 96-109)
- legislation exempting banks and savings and loan organizations from certain Federal Trade Commission requirements (P.L. 96-37)

- temporary authorization for lenders to exceed state usury ceilings, and for qualifying financial institutions to offer share drafts, automatic transfer services, and remote service units (P.L. 96-104, P.L. 96-161).

SIGNIFICANT LEGISLATION NOT ENACTED

Among the most significant legislation not passed during the first session of the 96th Congress were:

- hospital cost containment
- ratification of SALT II
- political action committee spending limitations
- congressional review of agency regulations
- synthetic fuel development
- national health insurance
- designation of a national holiday to honor Martin Luther King, Jr.
- lobbying disclosure
- Energy Mobilization Board and Priority Energy Projects
- corporate criminal liability for product defects
- Alaska lands
- airport noise control
- crude-oil windfall profits tax.

VETOES

President Carter vetoed one bill passed during 1979. The bill, vetoed on January 3, 1980, was S. 2096, which provided for a study by the secretary of health, education, and welfare of the long-term health effects in humans of exposure to dioxins. The president's decision was based on the inclusion of a legislative veto provision—the subject of a long-standing disagreement between the executive and legislative branches of government.

## Congress and Government

**Department of Education Organization Act** (P.L. 96-88). The new Department of Education created by this act will be larger than five other cabinet departments. With a budget exceeding $14 billion and a staff of over 17,000 employees, it consolidates more than 150 federal education programs formerly run by forty federal agencies. The goals of the act include improved access to educational and vocational opportunities, improved management of federal education programs, and increased accountability of federal education officials.

The measure was approved after protracted debate in the Congress. The main stumbling block was opponents' fears that the new department would result in increased federal intervention in and control of state and local education programs. As it was finally approved, the legislation does not authorize any new programs or abolish any existing ones, nor does it make any changes in existing educational law or policies. The federal government is expressly prohibited from coopting responsibilities of state, local, and tribal governments in the formulation and implementation of educational policy. Reflecting the antiinflationary mood of the country, the authorizing legislation mandates that the appropriations committees set annual ceilings on the number of staff employees, including experts and consultants.

The law authorizes six assistant secretaries in the following areas of education: elementary/secondary; postsecondary; vocational, community, and adult; special education and rehabilitative services; research and improvement; and civil rights. It also creates an Intergovernmental Advisory Council on Education to conduct studies and to advise the secretary and the president on educational policy. The council will also serve as a forum for the ideas and opinions of people outside the department. (S. 210: Sen. Ribicoff, D-Conn., and others; H.R. 2444: Rep. Brooks, D-Tex., and others.)

**Trade Reorganization Plan** (Reorganization Plan No. 3 of 1979). The Reorganization Plan No. 3 submitted by the Carter administration to realign foreign trade functions of the government was accepted by the Congress in early November. Such a plan takes effect automatically unless disapproved by either house within sixty days of submission. The reorganization was both a response to expected challenges in implementing the Multilateral Trade Negotiations (MTN) agreements, and a commitment to maintaining and improving the U.S. position in international trade. It places responsibility for the development, coordination, and negotiation of trade policy with the Office of the U.S. Trade Representative, formerly the Office of the Special Trade Representative. The Department of Commerce is charged with enhancing international competitiveness of American industry, with important new functions transferred to the new undersecretary for international trade.

Policy areas covered by the trade representative will include import remedies, East-West trade negotiations, international investment, commodity negotiations, energy trade, and export expansion. The trade representative will also take the lead in negotiations under the General Agreement on Tariffs and Trade, and on trade matters covered by the Organization for Economic Cooperation and Development and the United Nations Conference on Trade and Development. As the president's principal spokesman on trade, the trade representative will assume sole responsibility for areas formerly handled by a variety of agencies. Consolidating these functions under a single office is expected to provide a consistent approach to international trade.

Consistency and efficiency were also paramount concerns in assigning nonagricultural trade responsibilities to the Department of Commerce. The reorganization plan transfers administration of countervailing duties and anti-dumping statutes from the Treasury Department to Commerce. The Commerce Department will also take over commercial representation formerly handled by the State Department. The assistant secretary for trade policy and programs will oversee day-to-day implementation of MTN agreements. Consolidation of functions is expected to improve the U.S. position in international trade by clearly defining management responsibilities and lines of communication. The Commerce Department will also provide the statistical and analytical support for the formulation of trade policy by the president and the trade representative.

Although the reorganization plan falls short of Senate proposals for a separate Department of Trade, the two-pronged approach greatly simplifies lines of responsibility in the conduct of international trade. Placing policy functions under the single Office of the U.S. Trade Representative and consolidating its support services and administrative functions in the Department of Commerce, the plan emphasizes the political and economic importance the administration and Congress place on fostering international trade.

**Justice System Improvement Act of 1979** (P.L. 96-157). This legislation restructures the Law Enforcement Assistance Administration (LEAA) by creating two new agencies for research and statistical work and also a new Office of Justice Assistance, Research, and Statistics (OJARS) for administration and policy formulation. The OJARS will provide staff support and coordinate activities of the other three agencies.

The National Institute of Justice (NIJ) will be the research adjunct of the LEAA, with authority to conduct or authorize research projects, to make grants, and to provide fellowships and clinical internships. The NIJ will collect and disseminate information and will provide technical advice and assistance to federal, state, and local justice system agencies.

The Bureau of Justice Statistics (BJS) will collect and analyze data on crime and the correlates of crime, with special emphasis on the problems of state and local governments. It will recommend national standards for justice statistics and will coordinate its activities with state, national, and international justice agencies. Data gathered by the BJS may not be used for law enforcement or against a particular individual.

The creation of OJARS, BJS, and NIJ frees the LEAA to pursue its primary function of operating grant programs for states. Grants are divided into three categories: formula grants, discretionary grants, and national priority grants. Formula grants will be distributed to participating states and localities in blocks of $300,000. Additional funding will be determined either by the population of the state or by a four-part formula based on population, crime rates, criminal justice expenditures, and taxes. National priority grants are available to state and local governments for programs or projects that have been shown to be effective or innovative and that are likely to have a beneficial effect on criminal justice. A list of such priority programs will be designated by the director of OJARS and the administrator of the LEAA. Discretionary grants will be awarded for periods up to three years for projects that would not otherwise be undertaken. Funds for the fiscal year will be distributed to provide 80 percent to the formula grant program, and 10 percent to each of the other grant programs.

The legislation authorizes $800 million annually through 1983 for LEAA, OJARS, and the two new agencies: $750 million for LEAA and OJARS, and $25 million each for NIJ and BJS. The act also authorizes $25 million for the Office of Community Anti-Crime Programs. It stipulates further that, in addition to funds appropriated under the Juvenile Justice and Delinquency Prevention Act, 19.15 percent of all LEAA funds be applied to juvenile delinquency programs. Training and manpower development programs provided in the act include programs for prosecuting attorneys, state and local criminal justice personnel, criminal justice education, and FBI training of state and local personnel. The act also authorizes death benefits of $50,000 to survivors of law enforcement officers or firemen killed in the line of duty. (S. 241: Sen. Kennedy, D-Mass., and others; H.R. 2061: Reps. Rodino, D-N.J., Mazzoli, D-Ky., McClory, R-Ill.)

ENERGY AND ENVIRONMENT

**Emergency Energy Conservation Act of 1979** (P.L. 96-102). The Congress was reluctant to appear to vote for gas rationing, but recognized the pressing need for standby authority during an energy crisis. The bill that finally emerged stressed the authority and responsibility of the states in developing and imposing conservation measures, but left the president with the power to enforce these programs. The new law is also a response to a commitment to the International Energy Agency to reduce petroleum consumption. In becoming a party to this agreement, the United States agreed to develop a conservation plan with mandatory provisions to be imposed during a crisis.

Title I of the act addresses the controversial issue of gasoline and diesel fuel rationing. The president is required to submit a standby gas rationing plan to Congress for review within 120 days of enactment. The plan will include a description of measures taken to develop a rationing system, a timetable for its implementation, and cost estimates. It must distribute the shortfall of gasoline and diesel supplies equally among the states and take the needs of different groups of end-users into account as much as possible. The standby plan could be rejected only by a joint resolution of disapproval within thirty days of submission to Congress. If no action is taken within the thirty days, the plan is approved.

Although strong congressional action is required to disapprove the president's rationing plan, a presidential decision to impose rationing is subject to veto by either house. The Congress granted the president the authority to impose rationing in the event of a severe energy supply disruption—defined in the legislation as a projected 20 percent shortfall for at least thirty days of home heating oil, gasoline, and diesel fuel supplies—or to comply with the international energy program. The disruption is further defined as one that is not manageable by other emergency procedures, that is likely to persist, and that is expected to have a major adverse impact on the national health, safety, or economy. Rationing could also be imposed with less than a 20 percent shortage and for reasons other than meeting international energy program commitments, but Congress would have to approve the decision by concurrent resolution. This rationing authority would expire sixty days after congressional approval of the request. Rationing coupons would be distributed on a state-by-state basis, with all states receiving a nationwide uniform percentage reduction from base-period consumption.

The law directs the president to establish an emergency energy conservation program with monthly state and national targets for conservation. A plan will be designed for the federal government to achieve a percentage reduction equal to or greater than the national goals. The states would assume primary responsibility for responding to the conservation targets by developing individualized state plans. Governors would be encouraged to submit state plans to meet the targets before any crisis occurs. In the event of an energy emergency, a state would be required to submit a plan to the secretary of energy within forty-five days of publication of the targets. If no plan is submitted, or if a state's plan is not approved, the federal government would impose conservation measures. States having approved plans but failing to meet conservation targets would also be subject to federal standards, although federal measures could not be imposed on a state with an approved plan for ninety days ·and could not be imposed unless supply fell at least 8 percent short of demand. States may submit to the secretary of energy alternative plans to federal measures, thus allowing the states a second chance to meet federal standards. Violations of requirements of a state plan carry a civil penalty of $1,000 per violation.

In order to be approved, a state plan must be reasonably likely to achieve conservation targets. It must not place a disproportionate share of the burden on any one segment of the population or on interstate commerce. The plan must not violate federal law or impose a tax, tariff, or user fee. Odd-even gas purchasing plans may be implemented only for cars registered in that state or in contiguous states. Weekend gas station closings are prohibited unless they are part of closures implemented on a rotating basis.

Conservation targets would represent a nationally uniform flat percentage of the individual state's base-period consumption. The targets will refer to a specific energy source and will be set to minimize economic disruption. Base-period consumption for each state will be determined in a two-step process. The first step will be a mathematical calculation of state energy use, with a three-year growth adjustment. The second step involves an assessment of extenuating characteristics for the particular state, granting the president discretionary powers to minimize disruption of the economy and essential services.

A state may request judicial review of targets established by the president, of findings that the state has failed to meet targets, or of disapproval of the state's plan by the secretary of energy. The court of appeals must make every effort to expedite consideration of such a request, although it may not grant injunctive relief until a final judgment is rendered. Decisions of the court of appeals may be reviewed by the Supreme Court.

The new conservation law also contains provisions on temperature restrictions in buildings. States could request waivers on heating and cooling limits if they could demonstrate comparable energy savings by alternate methods. State and local governments would monitor compliance and implementation of these alternate methods. The law also authorizes the president to impose minimum fuel purchase requirements of $5, or $7 for eight-cylinder vehicles. The secretary of energy may raise minimums as he sees fit. Fines of $100 would be imposed for noncompliance. The act authorizes a study of commercial and industrial storage of fuel (hoarding) and establishes a program to monitor middle distillates.

By requiring strong congressional action to disapprove presidential action and by encouraging diverse state responses, the law seeks to provide a flexible framework that can be implemented quickly and equitably in an energy crisis. (S. 1030: Sens. Domenici, R-N.Mex., Johnston, D-La., Jackson, D-Wash.)

**Energy Appropriations: Low-Income Energy Assistance, Alternative Fuels, and Conservation** (P.L. 96-126). Congressional debate on funding for the Interior and Energy Departments and related agency activities was marked by regional bickering over the distribution of fuel aid to the poor and elderly. The appropriations legislation provides $1.35 billion in emergency fuel assistance, including $1.2 billion to be administered through the Department of Health, Education, and Welfare, and $150 million through the Community Services Administration (over and above the $250 million previously appropriated to CSA). Of the $1.6 billion total, $400 million is earmarked for distribution to Supplementary Security Income recipients not in Medicaid institutions as a one-time energy allowance not to exceed $250 per recipient. Checks including the one-time energy allowance will be sent to SSI recipients in January 1980. Any funds left over from the SSI distribution (because of the ceiling for individual payments) will be added to the $800 million earmarked for distribution as grants to the states to aid households in which income does not exceed 125 percent of the poverty level. These funds will be distributed either under a federally approved state plan or in accordance with an HEW plan. States may use funds to establish credit with sellers of fuel, to allocate more funds to households with higher energy costs, and so forth. Payments received under these energy allowance programs will not count as income or resources in determining eligibility for income-tested programs such as Aid to Families with Dependent Children, food stamps, and so forth.

The $400 million allocated for energy assistance to SSI recipients and the $400 million administered through the Community Services Administration (CSA) will be allotted among the states in accordance with the severity of the weather, energy usage, and energy costs. Emergency energy assistance covers energy-related costs but not weatherization expenses. Maximum payments under the program administered by the CSA are $400 per household in federal funds, but states may supplement this amount.

Appropriations for the Energy Department include $19 billion for an Energy Security Reserve to stimulate domestic production of alternative fuels such as coal, shale, tar sands, lignite, peat, biomass, solid waste, unconventional natural gas, and other fuels not made from crude oil. The appropriations legislation also establishes a $1 billion Solar and Conservation Reserve to be used to stimulate solar energy development and energy conservation. Both reserves are contingent on passage of authorizing legislation. However, approximately $2.2 billion in funds is available immediately for purchase or aid in the production of synthetic fuels and to support preliminary commercialization of alternative fuels. Fossil energy research and development programs received $746 million in appropriations and energy conservation programs received $628 million. Revenues from the so-called windfall profits tax, if enacted, are to be used to reimburse the Treasury for emergency fuel assistance payments, and it is contemplated funds from that tax will also be used to finance the reserves for the development of alternative fuels and solar energy and for energy conservation.  (H.R. 4930: Rep. Yates, D-Ill.)

FOREIGN POLICY AND INTERNATIONAL TRADE

**Taiwan Relations Act of 1979** (P.L. 96-8).  With the recognition of the People's Republic of China (mainland China) on January 1, 1979, the United States severed diplomatic relations with Taiwan.  The Taiwan Relations Act was enacted to maintain people-to-people contact with Taiwan.  It articulates U.S. policy on the importance of peace and stability in the Western Pacific and affirms a commitment to the security of Taiwan.  The act stipulates that the United States will provide defensive arms to Taiwan and will consider any attempt by the People's Republic of China to resolve the Taiwan issue by other than peaceful means as a matter "of grave concern."  The United States will regard Taiwan as a foreign country for the purposes of domestic law and eligibility for government programs, but the act is silent on the position of Taiwan in international law.  It does not affect the validity of international agreements between the United States and Taiwan in force before the recognition of mainland China.

The primary vehicle for maintaining relations between the two countries is the American Institute in Taiwan, a nonprofit corporation.  The institute is authorized to enter into agreements with the governing authorities of Taiwan on behalf of the president or U.S. government agencies.  The secretary of state will submit the text of any such agreement to Congress, unless this would endanger national security.  Under such circumstances, the agreements would be submitted to the foreign relations committees.  The agreements made by the institute are subject to the same congressional review and approval requirements they would have to meet if they were made by a government agency.  The secretary of state is also directed to submit a report every six months for a two-year period on economic relations between the two countries, "noting any interference with normal commercial relations."

Federal departments and agencies are authorized to provide property and services to the institute on a reimbursable basis.  Alien employees of the U.S. government in Taiwan will be transferred to the institute without loss of benefits.  Government employees will be separated from government service for the period of service with the institute, also without loss of rights or benefits upon reemployment by the government.

In dealing with the people of Taiwan, the president is directed to recognize an instrumentality established by Taiwan with powers to act on behalf of the citizens.  The president is authorized to extend to representatives of the Taiwan instrumentality immunities and privileges "necessary for the performance of their functions." This section precludes full diplomatic immunities and privileges.

10

The president is directed to inform the Congress of any danger to the security of Taiwan or to U.S. interests on Taiwan. This includes both military and nonmilitary threats from any external power. The president and the Congress would then determine appropriate action in accordance with constitutional processes. Defense-related sales to Taiwan will be reviewed by U.S. military authorities before a decision is reached by the president and Congress. Such sales would be authorized if the Congress and the president determine the arms are necessary for Taiwan to maintain a sufficient self-defense capability. (H.R. 2479: Rep. Zablocki, D-Wis., and others; S. 245: Sen. Church, D-Idaho.)

**Panama Canal Act of 1979** (P.L. 96-70). The Panama Canal Treaty of 1977 between the United States and the Republic of Panama went into effect on October 1, 1979. Legislation to implement conditions of the treaty was passed barely a week before this deadline, after prolonged and sometimes bitter debate. The Panama Canal Act establishes the framework for U.S. maintenance and operation of the canal. It defines the responsibilities and authority of the president in defending the canal area and formulates the personnel policies to be applied to U.S. government employees in the Canal Zone.

The act establishes the Panama Canal Commission as an executive agency under the direction of the president through the secretary of defense, with responsibility for the maintenance and operation of the canal. The commission is supervised by a board composed of nine members, at least five of whom must be U.S. nationals. One of the five must be the secretary of defense or his designate, and the other four must cast their votes as directed by the secretary of defense or his designate. Three U.S. nationals who are experts—one each in the areas of shipping, U.S. port operations, and U.S. labor relations—must be included on the board. Three members must be from the private sector, although these members need not be the three technical experts. All U.S. members will be appointed by the president, subject to Senate confirmation. Non-U.S. nationals on the board must be nationals of Panama. The commission will submit an annual financial report, as well as an annual review of operation and management.

The act establishes the positions of administrator, deputy administrator, chief engineer, and ombudsman within the Panama Canal Commission. In line with certain treaty provisions, a joint two-nation Commission on the Environment and a joint two-nation Sea Level Canal Study Committee are also authorized. The Consultative Committee established under the treaty will act as an international forum for the exchange of ideas between the United States and Panama on policies affecting the operation of the canal, but the committee will have no authority to direct the actions of the Panama Canal Commission.

The statute mandates that funds appropriated may not exceed the estimated total of toll.revenues from canal operation during that fiscal year plus any unexpended funds from prior fiscal years occurring after the effective date of the act. U.S. tax revenues may not be used to fulfill treaty obligations, unless specifically approved by Congress through the authorization and appropriation process. The law also states that all U.S. expenses for the maintenance and operation of the canal, and for related services such as health care and education, will be paid first, before making payments to Panama under treaty provisions. The president is prohibited from acceding to any interpretation of treaty provisions that would allow the Republic of Panama to tax retroactively U.S. citizens or businesses in the Canal Zone.

The law provides that the president may ensure the security of the canal and introduce U.S. military troops into the area if it is under armed attack or if it is his opinion that "conditions exist which threaten" canal security. In either event, the Panama Canal administrator would be required to accept defense-related orders from the U.S. military. This condition would apply even after 1990, when the administrator will be a Panamanian. The act also directs the president to enter into negotiations with the government of Panama on the stationing of U.S. military forces in the Canal Zone after the termination of the treaty in 1999. The president is forbidden to transfer the canal to Panama before the treaty deadline of 1999. Other properties will be transferred gradually to Panamanian ownership, as provided in the treaty. (H.R. 111: Reps. Murphy, D-N.Y., de la Garza, D-Tex., Hubbard, D-Ky.)

**Trade Agreements Act of 1979** (P.L. 96-39). The Multilateral Trade Negotiations (MTN) are an ongoing attempt by ninety-nine world trading partners to facilitate international trade by easing trade barriers, while accommodating the national interests of the parties involved. Under the General Agreement on Tariffs and Trade, seven rounds of trade negotiations have been held since 1948. The first five rounds concerned tariff reductions. The last two primarily dealt with "nontariff barriers"—national laws and policies that affect international trade.

The eleven titles of this act implement agreements reached at the Tokyo round of the MTN. The legislation amends the Trade Act of 1974 to bring U.S. law into conformance with these agreements. Under. the new law, the secretary of the treasury can impose countervailing duties for foreign subsidy of exports to this country or antidumping duties for sales to this country at less than fair value only if there is a threat of "material injury" to U.S. industry. This provision limits the authority of the secretary to protect U.S. producers. The law simplifies methods of determining customs value by establishing one primary method of valuation (transaction value) and four alternate methods. Government procurement policy will be changed to provide equal access to foreign producers. The president is authorized to waive certain "buy American" restrictions on government purchases for developing countries that provide reciprocal rights to U.S. products and for developed countries that are parties to the MTN agreements. A new standards code will discourage standards-setting that creates unnecessary obstacles to international trade, with producers encouraged to adopt existing international standards. Procedures for settling disputes will protect U.S. producers from unfair or unreasonable standards abroad and will afford similar protection to foreign producers. This title is expected to improve U.S. access to foreign markets where unduly severe standards had previously restricted such access.

The act provides for the implementation of certain tariff concessions agreed upon in the MTN, with cuts averaging 30 percent over the eight-year period beginning January 1, 1980. The act eliminates duties on civil aircraft, parts, and engines as required under the international Civil Aircraft Agreement. Import quotas on cheese and other dairy products are raised, considerably broadening foreign access to the U.S. market, and a floor of 1.2 billion pounds is set on meat imports. The method of computing duties on distilled spirits is changed from the wine-gallon method (duties levied on quantity) to the proof method (duties levied on alcohol content), thus bringing U.S. standards in line with international methods.

The president is authorized to impose sanctions on imports or take other action to protect U.S. producers and providers of services from unjustifiable or discriminatory foreign trade practices. This section is designed to enforce U.S. rights in areas not specifically covered by international trade agreements. Action can be initiated by the president on his own motion or on the recommendation of the special trade representative in response to a request from an interested party. This section also provides more information to private-sector parties on trade agreements, remedies, and foreign government policies.

The act provides greater opportunity for review and appeal of the secretary of the treasury's decisions on countervailing or antidumping duties and allows for judicial review of Customs Service decisions on appraised value or rate of duty. (H.R. 4537: Reps. Wright, D-Tex., Rhodes, R-Ariz.)

**Export Administration Act of 1979** (P.L. 96-72). The Export Administration Act of 1979 is an extension of export control authority and a revision of U.S. export policy as set by the Export Administration Act of 1969 (P.L. 91-184). The 1979 act emphasizes controls on the transfer of technology as distinct from products, reduces the number of controlled items, and establishes procedures for review and appeal of controls decisions. It supports the right of U.S. producers to engage in international commerce without unduly restrictive export prohibitions. Export of goods and technologies vital to national security interests will be evaluated under the "critical technology approach" developed by the Department of Defense. This provision will ease licensing restrictions on technologies that are not demonstrably critical to national security.

The act sets criteria for use by the president in establishing export controls and requires an annual review and report on his conclusions. Factors such as economic costs, alternative methods of achieving stated foreign policy goals, foreign availability of the product or products under consideration, and the effectiveness of controls must be taken into account in his decisions. In addition, the law establishes an Office of Foreign Product and Technology Assessment in the Department of Commerce as the centralized authority for determining availability to controlled countries of goods and technologies subject to U.S. export restrictions. Such assessments had been carried out formerly by individual agencies.

The act revises licensing procedures of the Department of Commerce to expedite routine cases, simplifies interagency review processes, and sets a 180-day limit within which all applications for export licenses must be approved or denied. An applicant denied a license would be informed of the statutory basis for the denial and would be permitted to appeal the decision.

In general, the legislation highlights the economic importance of increased U.S. export trade, while recognizing the responsibility to protect national security interests and further foreign policy objectives. (S. 737: Sens. Stevenson, D-Ill., and Heinz, R-Pa.; H.R. 4034: Rep. Bingham, D-N.Y., and others.)

**Shipping Act Amendments of 1979** (P.L. 96-25). This legislation duplicates a bill passed in the 95th Congress to give the Federal Maritime Commission (FMC) authority to combat rebating and other illegal price practices in international shipping by water. The 1978 amendments to the Shipping Act of 1916 were pocket-vetoed by President Carter, who felt passage of the bill would endanger ongoing negotiations on shipping problems with Japan and several European countries. Supporters of the bill asserted that restrictions on rebating could not be enforced against foreign shippers by the FMC without remedial legislation.

The law requires carriers, forwarders, shippers, and others covered in the act to state under oath that, among other things, they do not engage in rebating, that they have taken positive steps to prevent the practice, and that they will file any information requested in an FMC investigation. Civil penalties of $5,000 per day must be assessed for failure to file this certificate. The statute increases civil penalties for illegal rebating from $5,000 to $25,000, and it authorizes the FMC to suspend for up to one year the tariffs of carriers found to be in violation. Any carrier who accepts cargo under a suspended tariff may be assessed a civil penalty of not more than $50,000 per shipment. A ten-day period is allowed for the president to disapprove a suspension for reasons of national defense or foreign policy.

For the first time, foreign carriers will be required to comply with FMC subpoenas and discovery orders. If a foreign-flag carrier claims the laws of a foreign country prevent cooperation with the FMC, the secretary of state is directed to negotiate with the foreign government to obtain the information requested. The act also prohibits the use of federal conspiracy statutes to punish illegal rebating committed after August 29, 1972. (S. 199: Sen. Inouye, D-Hawaii; H.R. 3055: Rep. Murphy, D-N.Y., and others.)

GOVERNMENT REGULATION

**Milwaukee Railroad Restructuring Act** (P.L. 96-101). When the Milwaukee Railroad filed for bankruptcy in December 1977, rail service to the Pacific Northwest became an endangered species. The bankruptcy court had ordered the shutdown of about half of the 9,800 miles of the system the day before the emergency legislation was passed, even as legislators from grain and coal states in the Pacific Northwest warned of the grave economic consequences such an interruption in service would cause. Under earlier general legislation, the Interstate Commerce Commission (ICC) could require "directed service" over abandoned lines during reorganization, at great cost to the taxpayer. The ICC also had the power to authorize abandonments and sales. The new law provides a more efficient, less costly method of railroad reorganization, and it affords a high level of protection to employees whose jobs are endangered or eliminated by the restructuring.

The law encourages the submission by employees, shippers, and national railway labor organizations of a plan to convert all or part of the Milwaukee system into a company owned by employees or by employees and shippers. The ICC will rule on the feasibility of the plan within thirty days. No prospect of federal funding will be considered in determining the financial feasibility of the employee-shipper ownership plan. If the plan does not prove feasible, the trustee of the railroad may immediately begin reorganization by selling or abandoning lines, subject to the approval of the bankruptcy court and an expedited ICC review. The court may authorize purchasers to operate interim service over the lines to be purchased. (In December the ICC rejected a proposal by an employee-shipper group—the New Milwaukee Lines, or NewMil—citing overly optimistic estimates of operating losses. The decision clears the way for the Milwaukee Railroad trustee to begin restructuring by eliminating unprofitable lines.)

The railroad and its employee organization must submit an employee protection agreement within twenty days of enactment of the legislation. If they fail to reach an agreement, the National Mediation Board will have twenty days to mediate the dispute. If the parties are still unable to reach a compromise, the law directs them to enter immediately into a "fair and equitable" employee protection agreement as prescribed by this legislation. The act provides $75 million in guarantees for employee severance benefits. The loans would be assigned a high priority among creditors of the Milwaukee bankruptcy estate. This agreement would supersede any traditional severance benefits plan.

Until a reorganization is completed or is found to be infeasible, the railroad will receive loan guarantees for operating funds from the ICC's

15

directed service account. The railroad is directed to maintain its entire system and to provide no less than its regular level of service. It may not embargo any traffic or abandon any service. In addition to government loans for operating expenses, large sums are set aside for furloughed or displaced railroad employees. The act authorizes $5 million for supplementary unemployment insurance, $1.5 million for new career training assistance, and $75 million for guarantees of employee severance claims. The government will also guarantee loans to railroads seeking to buy or rehabilitate Milwaukee lines.

The legislation minimizes the role of the ICC in this railroad bankruptcy proceeding and replaces federal expenditures with loan guarantees. Government involvement in the actual restructuring of the railroad is also minimized. (S. 1905: Sens. Cannon, D-Nev., Long, D-La., Packwood, R-Oreg.)

**Chrysler Corporation Loan Guarantee Act of 1979** (P.L. 96-185). In the final hours of the 1979 session, Congress approved a bill authorizing $1.5 billion in federal loan guarantees for the financially crippled Chrysler Corporation. The total aid package—the largest ever for a private corporation— came to over $3.5 billion.

The Chrysler Corporation Loan Guarantee Board will approve guarantees under this act. The board will consist of the secretary of the treasury, the chairman of the Federal Reserve, and the comptroller general. The secretaries of labor and transportation will serve as nonvoting members. Commitments to guarantee Chrysler payments of principal and interest on new loans can be made only if the board determines that: (1) Chrysler adopts energy-saving features in its automobile designs; (2) failure to make the commitment would seriously affect the economy and employment; (3) Chrysler submits an operating plan demonstrating its ability to continue as a going concern after December 31, 1983, without federal assistance; (4) Chrysler submits a financing plan including $1.43 billion in guaranteed assistance from sources other than the federal government; (5) the financing from nonfederal sources is available and adequate to meet projected needs during the period covered by the financing plan; (6) Chrysler creditors waive the right to recover under any prior credit commitment that may be in default; (7) no current credit may be converted to federally guaranteed financing; and (8) the financing plan contributes to Chrysler's domestic economic viability.

The board may issue commitments to guarantee loans once it has adequate assurance of the availability of the required $1.43 billion in guaranteed concessions and assistance from nonfederal sources. Actual guarantees will not be issued in any amount unless the nonfederal contribution is in hand to match dollar for dollar the amount guaranteed by the board.

All federally guaranteed loans must be secured, and the federal government will have first priority among creditors. It may waive first priority in favor of state and local governments and may agree to accept equal priority for up to $100,000 of the claim of any supplier and up to $400 million of the claim of any creditor providing new nonfederally guaranteed loans.

A stumbling block in preparing the final bill was the amount of wage and benefit concessions to be required of Chrysler employees. The compromise version includes concessions in the amount of $462.5 million over three years for union employees and $125 million for nonunion personnel. The union figures include $203 million in concessions already contained in the contract between Chrysler and the United Auto Workers. A new agreement will have to be negotiated to accommodate the concessions.

The Chrysler Corporation may not pay dividends on its stocks until all federally guaranteed loans are repaid. The deadline for full repayment of such loans is December 31, 1990.

Chrysler is directed to establish an employee stock ownership plan as a condition of receiving guarantees. The company will issue $162.5 million worth of new common stock to its employees in lieu of wage increases. An additional $100 million in stocks will be available for sale to employees. The accompanying table shows the breakdown of the $3.5 billion package passed by Congress. The components of the $1.43 billion in nonfederally guaranteed aid may be modified by the board, as long as the aggregate amount remains the same. (H.R. 5860: Rep. Moorhead, D-Pa., and others; S. 2094: Sen. Proxmire, D-Wis.)

CHRYSLER CORPORATION AID

(millions of dollars)

| | |
|---|---:|
| *In order to obtain:* | |
| Federally guaranteed loans | 1,500.0 |
| *Chrysler must arrange:* | |
| Nonfederally guaranteed assistance | |
|    New credit or concessions from U.S. banks | 500.0 |
|    New credit from foreign banks | 150.0 |
|    Concessions from state, local, and other governments | 250.0 |
|    Concessions from suppliers and dealers | 180.0 |
|    Sale of equity securities | 50.0 |
|    Sale of assets | 300.0 |
|    Total | 1,430.0 |
| *The legislation also requires:* | |
| Wage and benefit concessions from union employees | 462.5 |
| Wage and benefit concessions from nonunion employees | 125.0 |
|    Total aid to Chrysler | 3,517.5 |

SOURCE: *Congressional Record*, December 20, 1979, pp. H12481-82.

**Food Stamps** (P.L. 96-58). Extraordinarily high rates of food price inflation and a large influx of new recipients combined to create an emergency situation in the food stamp program in 1979. By midyear it was evident that expenditures were rapidly approaching the ceiling set on 1979 appropriations. The only option available under the 1977 legislation was an across-the-board flat percentage reduction in benefits, with the possibility of a total shutdown of the program. Legislation was necessary to increase appropriations for the fiscal year and to make changes in other provisions of the 1977 law that were creating undue hardship for some recipients.

The new law raises funding limits for the program by $620 million to approximately $6.8 billion. It requires the secretary of agriculture to file monthly reports on the monthly and cumulative costs of the program, including an assessment of whether an insufficiency of funds will necessitate benefit reductions. If a shortfall is predicted, the secretary must take action within sixty days to reduce benefits. The secretary will then report to the congressional agriculture committees on the reason for the reduction, the methods employed to achieve the reduction, and the action already taken in reducing allotments. He is also directed to establish minimum allotments if reductions are implemented. Benefit reductions may be made on a basis other than flat percentage, allowing the secretary to scale reductions for the benefit of lower-income recipients.

The new law takes particular notice of the special difficulties of elderly and disabled recipients of food stamps. These population groups were especially hard hit by provisions of the 1977 law restricting deductions for medical and shelter expenses. The 1979 act provides an excess medical expense deduction for households with an elderly or disabled person. The deduction covers allowable medical expenses over $35 a month, and it is adjusted for inflation semiannually. The ceiling on the amount of excess shelter expense is also removed.

There are several changes in information requirements and enforcement provisions. Recipients may be required to furnish their social security numbers in order to receive benefits, and this information can be used in investigations of household eligibility. Recipients who have fraudulently obtained food stamps will not be eligible to reenter the program unless they agree to reimburse the government for their illegal gains, either by taking a reduction in benefits or by repaying in cash the value of fraudulently obtained coupons. Failure to meet the repayment schedule will result in appropriate allotment reductions. The state will be entitled to 50 percent of recoveries made in accordance with these procedures.

The act broadens eligibility by including blind or disabled persons in group living arrangements. It denies benefits to workers on strike unless their households meet income, assets, and work registration requirements of the act. (H.R. 4057: Rep. Richmond, D-N.Y.; S. 1309: Sens. Talmadge, D-Ga., McGovern, D-S. Dak., Dole, R-Kans.)

**Federal Magistrate Act of 1979** (P.L. 96-82).  The position of magistrate was created in 1968 to replace the position of U.S. commissioner.  Since that time, heavy caseloads have produced pressure to expand the jurisdiction of federal magistrates.  Under the new law, magistrates can decide civil cases, preside at jury trials, and assume expanded powers in criminal cases.  Magistrates are authorized to handle any federal misdemeanor (an offense with a maximum one-year jail sentence), regardless of the amount of the fine or the complexity of the case.  Formerly, magistrates could only hear misdemeanor cases where the fine was under $1,000 and where the accused consented to trial by a magistrate and waived the right to a jury trial.  Consent by the accused is still required, but waiver of the right to a jury trial is no longer necessary.

The statute requires the issuance of court rules to ensure voluntary consent by involved parties to a jury trial.  It also provides for appeal of the magistrate's decision to the circuit court of appeals or to a district court judge, if the parties consent at time of referral.

The Judicial Conference of the United States is required to establish standards for magistrate evaluation and selection procedures.  Public notice of magistrate vacancies is also mandated.  The conference will establish a merit selection panel to review candidates for full-time positions.  (S. 237: Sen. DeConcini, D-Ariz.; H.R. 1046: Rep. Kastenmeier, D-Wis., and others.)

Under procedures established by the Congressional Budget and Impoundment Control Act of 1974 (P.L. 93-344), the Congress adopted two concurrent resolutions on the budget for fiscal year 1980 (October 1, 1979 to September 30, 1980).

The first resolution, H. Con. Res. 107, was passed May 24, 1979. It specifies target levels for subsequent congressional action on total budget authority, revenues, outlays, the deficit, and the public debt.

The second resolution, S. Con. Res. 53, sets binding limits on the five categories listed above. These limits cannot be violated unless the Congress adopts a third budget resolution. Although the second concurrent resolution includes a provision expressing the sense of the Congress that such action should be avoided if at all possible, some observers feel that economic conditions and overly optimistic budget estimates may necessitate a rare third resolution in the spring of 1980.

The second concurrent resolution was adopted November 28, 1979, nearly two months after the start of the fiscal year to which it pertains. Final approval was delayed by lengthy conference consideration of a controversial "reconciliation" proposal, which would have required certain committees to make $3.6 billion in spending cuts to stay within limits set by the budget resolution. Mandatory savings were replaced in the final version with non-binding language urging "maximum restraint" and "maximum effort toward

### TABLE 1

#### Budget Totals, Fiscal Year 1980
(billions of dollars)

| | *First Concurrent Resolution Targets* | *Second Concurrent Resolution Binding Totals* | *President's Estimates* [a] |
|---|---|---|---|
| Budget authority | 604.4 | 638.0 | |
| Outlays | 532.0 | 547.6 | 547.1 |
| Revenues | 509.0 | 517.8 | 513.9 |
| Budget deficit | 23.0 | 29.8 | 33.2 |
| Public debt | 887.2 | 886.4 | n.a. |

[a] Revised 1980 budget estimates released by the Office of Management and Budget, October 1979. Data for public debt are not available.

Source: U.S. Congress, Congressional Budget Office.

savings." Reaching a compromise on increased spending for defense and social programs also slowed the approval process.

The 1980 budget is billed as a "tight," "no-fat" budget, with outlays increasing only 11 percent over 1979 levels, before adjusting for inflation (13.3 percent for calendar year 1979). Table 1 presents budget totals from the first and second resolutions for fiscal year 1980, along with the administration's October estimates of the 1980 budget. Revenues are estimated $8.8 billion higher and outlays are set $15.6 billion higher in the second resolution than they had been in the first. As a result, the budget deficit estimated in the second concurrent resolution is $6.8 billion higher than the one contained in the first concurrent resolution.

TABLE 2

SUMMARY, BY FUNCTION, OF CONGRESSIONAL ACTION ON BUDGET
OUTLAYS FOR FISCAL YEAR 1980
(billions of dollars)

| | Second Concurrent Resolution | | |
| | Dollar | Percentage | Current |
| *Function* | limit | of total | *Level* |
|---|---|---|---|
| National defense | 129.9 | 23.7 | 129.6 |
| International affairs | 8.4 | 1.5 | 8.3 |
| General science, space, and technology | 5.7 | 1.0 | 5.7 |
| Energy | 7.2 | 1.3 | 6.8 |
| National resources and environment | 11.9 | 2.2 | 11.9 |
| Agriculture | 2.6 | 0.5 | 2.1 |
| Commerce and housing credit | 2.8 | 0.5 | 2.9 |
| Transportation | 18.6 | 3.4 | 18.8 |
| Community and regional development | 8.4 | 1.5 | 8.1 |
| Education, training, employment, and social services | 31.0 | 5.7 | 30.4 |
| Health | 54.4 | 9.9 | 56.3 |
| Income security | 190.0 | 34.7 | 188.4 |
| Veterans' benefits and services | 20.8 | 3.8 | 20.8 |
| Administration of justice | 4.4 | 0.8 | 4.5 |
| General government | 4.2 | 0.8 | 4.4 |
| General purpose fiscal assistance | 9.0 | 1.7 | 8.6 |
| Interest | 58.1 | 10.6 | 58.0 |
| Allowances | − 0.2 | a | 0.7 |
| Undistributed offsetting receipts | −19.7 | − 3.6 | −19.6 |
| Total | 547.6 | 100.0 | 546.9 |

a Less than 0.1 percent.
SOURCE: U.S. Congress, Congressional Budget Office.

The administration and the Congress are in close agreement over the 1980 budget. The administration's estimate of revenues is only $3.9 billion (or 0.8 percent) lower than the estimate in the second concurrent resolution, and its outlay estimate is only $0.5 billion lower. By way of contrast, the administration a year ago estimated revenues and outlays in the 1979 budget $4.0 billion (0.9 percent) higher than the Congress.

Table 2 shows budget outlays in the nineteen functional categories specified in the budget, along with the outlays that will result from congressional actions taken during the first session. Increases in national defense and income security programs account for $12.4 billion of the rise in outlays from the first to the second resolution. Senate conferees found that their demands for higher defense spending would be met only if they conceded similar increases in social programs. National defense spending as a percentage of total outlays rose from 23.0 percent in 1979 to 23.7 percent in 1980, and income security spending increased from 32.7 to 34.7 percent. Interest rose from 9.8 to 10.6 percent, while agriculture dropped from 1.5 to 0.5 percent. Changes in percentage share of total budget outlays from 1979 to 1980 were minimal in most other cases.

Legislation that affects outlays, of course, is not typically drawn up along the lines of the functional categories in the budget. There is, for example, no single appropriation bill for national defense. Rather, outlays and budget authority for national defense are the total of the amounts provided for in many different pieces of legislation. The same is true of the other functional categories. Most congressional decisions on specific amounts for budget authority and outlays result from actions taken by the House and Senate Appropriations Committees, the House Ways and Means Committee, or the Senate Finance Committee. Table 3 summarizes congressional action on 1980 budget outlays by committee.

---

### TABLE 3
ACTION ON 1980 BUDGET OUTLAYS BY COMMITTEE
(millions of dollars)

| Committee | Second Concurrent Resolution | Current Level |
|---|---|---|
| House of Representatives | | |
| Agriculture | 1,484 | 1,136 |
| Appropriations | 343,105 | 341,483 |
| Armed Services | −114 | −139 |
| Banking, Finance, and Urban Affairs | −1,395 | −1,404 |
| District of Columbia | 9 | 9 |

*(Table continued on next page)*

TABLE 3 (continued)

| Committee | Second Concurrent Resolution | Current Level |
|---|---|---|
| Education and Labor | 32 | 32 |
| Foreign Affairs | 9,664 | 9,664 |
| Government Operations | 6,864 | 6,864 |
| House Administration | 57 | 59 |
| Interior and Insular Affairs | 953 | 951 |
| Interstate and Foreign Commerce | 4,844 | 4,859 |
| Judiciary | 164 | 164 |
| Merchant Marine and Fisheries | 123 | −317 |
| Post Office and Civil Service | 21,710 | 21,807 |
| Public Works and Transportation | 1,884 | 1,884 |
| Science and Technology | 18 | 18 |
| Small Business | 0 | 0 |
| Veterans Affairs | 620 | 623 |
| Ways and Means | 233,266 | 234,441 |
| Not allocated by committee | −75,685 | −75,220 |
| Total | 547,600 | 546,911 |
| Senate | | |
| Agriculture | 1,372 | 1,011 |
| Appropriations | 343,100 | 341,483 |
| Armed Services | −549 | −520 |
| Banking, Housing, and Urban Affairs | −1,559 | −1,568 |
| Commerce, Science, and Transportation | −2 | −2 |
| Energy and Natural Resources | 940 | 940 |
| Environment and Public Works | 2,062 | 2,012 |
| Finance | 239,945 | 241,217 |
| Foreign Relations | 9,663 | 9,663 |
| Governmental Affairs | 21,808 | 21,808 |
| Judiciary | 165 | 165 |
| Labor and Human Resources | 4,867 | 4,867 |
| Rules and Administration | 57 | 59 |
| Veterans' Affairs | 785 | 788 |
| Indian Affairs | 208 | 208 |
| Small Business | 0 | 0 |
| Not allocated by committee | −75,263 | −75,220 |
| Total | 547,600 | 546,911 |

SOURCE: U.S. Congress, Congressional Budget Office.

# APPENDIXES

# Appendix A

## History of Bills Enacted into Public Law, 1979

(Cross-reference of bill numbers to public laws may be found in Appendix B.)

| Title | Bill No. | Date introduced | Committee | | Date reported | | Report No. | | Page of passage in Congressional Record | | Date of passage | | Public Law | |
|---|---|---|---|---|---|---|---|---|---|---|---|---|---|---|
| | | | House | Senate | House | Senate | House | Senate | House | Senate | House | Senate | Date approved | No. |
| To extend from January 22 to January 29, 1979, the time for the filing the Economic Report. | H.J. Res. 1 | Jan. 15 | .......... | .......... | .......... | .......... | .......... | .......... | H 16 | S 214 | Jan. 15 | Jan. 18 | Jan. 22 | 96–1 |
| Authorizing the Administrator of General Services to conduct future sales of the Carson City silver dollars under such terms and conditions as he deems proper. | H.R. 1902 | Feb. 8 | | | | | | | H 567 | S 1778 | Feb. 13 | Feb. 26 | Mar. 7 | 96–2 |
| Repealing the section relative to financial privacy of P.L. 95–630, to extend the authority for flexible regulation of interest rates on deposits and accounts in depository institutions. | S. 37 | Jan. 15 | BFUA | BHUA | .......... | Feb. 9 | .......... | 96–5 | H 902 | S 1409 | Feb. 27 | Feb. 9 | Mar. 7 | 96–3 |
| Making certain administrative changes which arose from the redrawing of the Federal judicial districts in the State of Illinois. | H.R. 2301 (S. 443) | Feb. 21 | Jud | Jud | Mar. 29 | Mar. 14 | 96–55 | 96–34 | H 1589 | S 3293 | Mar. 22 | Mar. 22 | Mar. 30 | 96–4 |
| Increasing through September 30, 1979, the Public Debt limit. | H.R. 2534 | Mar. 1 | WM | .......... | Mar. 8 | .......... | 96–31 | .......... | H 1373 | S 3456 | Mar. 15 | Mar. 27 | Apr. 2 | 96–5 |
| To extend temporarily the authority of the Secretary of the Treasury to waive the imposition of the countervailing duties. | H.R. 1147 | Jan. 18 | WM | Fin | Feb. 22 | Mar. 22 | 96–15 | 96–45 | H 1018 | S 3580 | Mar. 1 | Mar. 28 | Apr. 5 | 96–6 |
| To rescind certain budget authority stated in the message of the President of January 31, 1979. | H.R. 2439 | Feb. 27 | App | App BUD | Mar. 1 | Mar. 8 | 96–25 | 96–33 | H 1093 | S 2705 | Mar. 6 | Mar. 14 | Apr. 9 | 96–7 |
| To promote the foreign policy of the United States through the maintenance of commercial, cultural, and other relations with the people on Taiwan on an unofficial basis. | H.R. 2479 (S. 245) | Feb. 28 | FA | FR | Mar. 3 | Mar. 1 | 96–26 | 96–7 | H 1288 | S 2667 | Mar. 13 | Mar. 13 | Apr. 10 | 96–8 |
| Reaffirming the United States commitment to the North Atlantic Alliance. | H.J. Res. 283 (S.J. Res. 54) | Mar. 28 | .......... | .......... | .......... | .......... | .......... | .......... | H 1935 | S 4106 | Apr. 4 | Apr. 5 | Apr. 19 | 96–9 |
| Increasing funds for and extending the life of the Council on Wage and Price Stability. | H.R. 2283 (S. 349) | Feb. 21 | BFUA | BHUA | Mar. 12 | Mar. 14 | 96–33 | 96–36 | H 1546 | S 3769 | Mar. 21 | Apr. 2 | May 10 | 96–10 |
| Authorizing the President to proclaim May 18, 1979, as "National Museum Day". | H.J. Res. 262 (S.J. Res. 62) | Mar. 20 | .......... | Jud | .......... | May 16 | .......... | .......... | H 3132 | S 6118 | May 15 | May 16 | May 18 | 96–11 |
| To confer certain powers on the Presidential Commission appointed to investigate the Three Mile Island nuclear powerplant accident. | S.J. Res. 80 | May 17 | .......... | .......... | .......... | .......... | .......... | .......... | H 3480 | S 6184 | May 21 | May 17 | May 23 | 96–12 |
| Authorizing the President to proclaim the week of May 6 through 12, 1979, as "National Historic Preservation Week". | S.J. Res. 71 | May 2 | .......... | .......... | .......... | .......... | .......... | .......... | H 3025 | S 5158 | May 10 | May 2 | May 24 | 96–13 |
| Authorizing the President to present on behalf of the Congress a specially struck gold medal to John Wayne. | S. 631 (H.R. 3767) | Mar. 13 | BFUA | BHUA | .......... | May 1 | .......... | 96–110 | H 3613 | S 5273 | May 23 | May 3 | May 26 | 96–15 |
| Authorizing $185 million for fiscal year 1979 for supplemental funds for NASA. | H.R. 1787 | Feb. 1 | ST | CST | Mar. 19 | May 10 | 96–53 | 96–128 | H 1749 | S 6147 | Mar. 28 | May 17 | June 4 | 96–16 |
| Authorizing $4.3 million for fiscal year 1980 for the Ocean Pollution Research Development and Monitoring Planning Act. | H.R. 2520 (S. 1122) | Feb. 28 | MMF ST | CST | May 1 May 1 | May 11 | 96–110 | 96–132 | H 3075 | S 6145 | May 14 | May 17 | June 4 | 96–17 |
| To authorize Federal Reserve banks to lend certain obligations to the Secretary of the Treasury to meet the short-term cash requirements of the Treasury. | H.R. 3404 | Apr. 3 | BFUA | .......... | May 1 | .......... | 96–111 | .......... | H 3659 | S 6765 | May 23 | May 24 | June 8 | 96–18 |
| Making technical and conforming changes to the financial disclosure provisions in the Ethics in Government Act. | H.R. 2805 | Mar. 13 | Jud POCS R | GA | May 2 May 2 | .......... | 96–114 | .......... | H 3078 | S 6521 | May 14 | May 23 | June 13 | 96–19 |

| Purpose | Bill No. | Date | H. Comm. | S. Comm. | Date | Date | Report | Report | H No. | S No. | Date | Date | Date | Pub. Law |
|---|---|---|---|---|---|---|---|---|---|---|---|---|---|---|---|
| Veterans' Administration. | (H.R. 1608) | Jan. 13 | VA | VA | May 10 | Apr. 27 | 96–140 | 96–100 | H 3466 | S 6041 | May 21 | May 16 | June 13 | 96–22 |
| Authorizing $1,391,593,000 for fiscal year 1980 for the U.S. Coast Guard. | S. 709<br>(H.R. 2295) | Mar. 21 | MMF | CST | May 4 | May 11 | 96–118 | 96–134 | H 3959 | S 6145 | May 31 | May 17 | June 13 | 96–23 |
| To defer from July 1, 1979 to May 1, 1980, the effective date of automatic termination insurance coverage for multiemployer pension plans. | H.R. 3915 | May 3 | EdL | ........ | May 23 | ........ | 96–215 | ........ | H 4004 | S 7013 | June 4 | June 6 | June 19 | 96–24 |
| To strengthen the Federal Maritime Commission's authority to deal with illegal rebating practices in U.S. waterborne foreign trade. | S. 199<br>(H.R. 3055) | Jan. 23 | MMF | CST | June 4 | May 15 | 96–232 | 96–147 | H 4009 | S 6515 | June 4 | May 23 | June 19 | 96–25 |
| Authorizing funds for fiscal years 1980 and 1981 for the National Advisory Committee on Oceans and Atmosphere. | H.R. 3577<br>(S. 951) | Apr. 10 | MMF | CST | May 3 | May 11 | 96–116 | 96–131 | H 3079 | S 6833 | May 14 | June 4 | June 21 | 96–26 |
| Authorizing $22 million to provide for an independent audit of the financial condition of the government of the District of Columbia. | H.R. 3879<br>(H.R. 3672)<br>(S. 905) | May 2 | DC | GA | May 8<br>May 9 | May 14 | 96–130<br>96–131 | 96–139 | H 3429 | S 6630 | May 17 | May 24 | June 21 | 96–27 |
| Clarifying ethical standards for Federal employees....... | S. 869 | Apr. 4 | Jud | ........ | May 2 | ........ | 96–115 | ........ | H 3689 | S 4241 | May 24 | Apr. 9 | June 22 | 96–28 |
| Authorizing supplemental funds for fiscal year 1979 for the defense establishment. | S. 429<br>(H.R. 2575) | Feb. 9 | AS | AS | Apr. 6 | Apr. 6 | 96–90 | 96–62 | H 3948 | S 5271 | May 31 | May 3 | June 27 | 96–29 |
| To extend the antitrust exemption for oil companies participating on an international energy program. | S. 1317 | June 12 | ........ | ENR | ........ | June 26 | ........ | ........ | H 5457 | S 8515 | June 28 | June 26 | June 30 | 96–30 |
| To provide authority for the waiver or reduction of penalties where peanuts are marketed in excess of the farm poundage quota. | S. 984<br>(H.R. 3575) | Apr. 23 | Agr | Agr | May 23 | May 4 | 96–213 | 96–118 | H 5037 | S 5707 | June 25 | May 10 | July 7 | 96–31 |
| To correct an error made in the printing of Public Law 95–613, authorizing funds through fiscal year 1983 for programs administered under the Family Planning Services and Population Research Act. | S.J. Res. 14 | Jan. 18 | IFC | ........ | May 15 | ........ | 96–187 | ........ | H 5049 | S 257 | June 25 | Jan. 18 | July 10 | 96–32 |
| Authorizing the Secretary of Health, Education, and Welfare to extend conditional designations of State health planning and development agencies. | H.R. 4556 | June 21 | | | | | | | H 5051 | S 8646 | June 25 | June 27 | July 16 | 96–33 |
| Congratulating the men and women of the Apollo program upon the tenth anniversary of the first manned landing on the Moon and requesting the President to proclaim the period of July 16 through July 24, 1979, as "United States Space Observance". | H.J. Res. 353<br>(S.J. Res. 77) | June 5 | POCS | Jud | July 9 | July 10 | 96–320 | 96–240 | H 5622 | S 9329 | July 10 | July 12 | July 17 | 96–34 |
| Authorizing funds for military and economic assistance to Israel and the Arab Republic of Egypt. | S. 1007<br>(H.R. 4035) | Apr. 25 | FA | FR | May 15 | May 2 | 96–161 | 96–113 | H 3897 | S 5755 | May 30 | May 14 | July 20 | 96–35 |
| Authorizing funds for fiscal year 1980 for future development of the area south of the original Smithsonian Institution Building, adjacent to Independence Avenue at Tenth Street, Southwest, in the City of Washington. | S. 927<br>(H.R. 3504) | Apr. 9 | HA | RAdm | ........ | May 14 | ........ | 96–140 | H 5509 | S 6251 | July 9 | May 21 | July 20 | 96–36 |
| To exempt Savings and Loan Associations from the jurisdiction of the Federal Trade Commission. | H.R. 3978 | May 7 | BFUA<br>IFC | ........ | June 12 | ........ | 96–265 | ........ | H 5516 | S 9115 | July 9 | July 10 | July 23 | 96–37 |
| Making supplemental appropriations for the fiscal year ending September 30, 19 9. | H.R. 4289 | May 31 | App | App | May 31 | June 18 | 96–227 | 96–224 | H 4107 | S 8514 | June 6 | June 26 | July 25 | 96–38 |
| To approve and implement the trade agreements negotiated by the United States in the Tokyo Round of Multilateral Trade Negotiations (MTN). | H.R. 4537 | June 19 | WM | Fin | July 3 | July 17 | 96–317 | 96–249 | H 5690 | S 10340 | July 11 | July 23 | July 26 | 96–39 |
| Increasing the annual authorization for the Navajo-Hopi Relocation Commission. | H.R. 3661 | Apr. 23 | IIA | ........ | May 10 | ........ | 96–134 | ........ | H 5921 | S 9639 | July 16 | July 17 | July 30 | 96–40 |
| To revise and update the Strategic and Critical Materials Stock Piling Act to conform the law to current stockpile policies and strengthen the role of Congress in stockpile matters. | H.R. 2154 | Feb. 15 | AS | AS | Mar. 15 | June 6 | 96–46 | 96–201 | H 1430 | S 7545 | Mar. 19 | June 13 | July 30 | 96–41 |
| To delay conditionally the effective date of certain rules of procedure and evidence proposed by the U.S. Supreme Court. | H.R. 4712 | July 10 | | | | | | | H 6375 | S 10460 | July 23 | July 24 | July 31 | 96–42 |
| To expedite trials of persons charged with Federal crimes. | S. 961 | Apr. 10 | Jud | Jud | July 26 | June 13 | 96–390 | 96–212 | H 6925 | S 8026 | July 31 | June 19 | Aug. 2 | 96–43 |
| Authorizing funds for activities of the National Science Foundation for fiscal year 1980. | H.R. 2729<br>(S. 527) | Mar. 8 | ST | LHR | Mar. 21 | May 1 | 96–61 | 96–107 | H 1716 | S 5490 | Mar. 27 | May 8 | Aug. 2 | 96–44 |
| Recognizing the anniversaries of the Warsaw uprising and the Polish resistance to the invasion of Poland during World War II. | H.J. Res. 373 | June 28 | ........ | FR | ........ | July 20 | ........ | ........ | H 5985 | S 10407 | July 16 | July 23 | Aug. 3 | 96–45 |

| Title | Bill No. | Date introduced | Committee | | Date reported | | Report No. | | Page of passage in Congressional Record | | Date of passage | | Public Law | |
|---|---|---|---|---|---|---|---|---|---|---|---|---|---|---|
| | | | House | Senate | House | Senate | House | Senate | House | Senate | House | Senate | Date approved | No. |
| Making technical corrections and clarifying certain amendments in certain education laws contained in the Education Amendments of 1978. | H.R. 4591 | June 22 | EdL | | July 13 | | 96-338 | | H 6381 | S 10461 | July 23 | July 24 | Aug. 6 | 96-46 |
| Authorizing funds for fiscal year 1980 for international affairs programs of the Department of the Treasury. | S. 976 (H.R. 3347) | Apr. 23 | BFUA | BHUA | May 15 | May 15 | 96-152 | 96-170 | H 4244 | S 6304 | June 8 | May 22 | Aug. 8 | 96-47 |
| Authorizing funds for fiscal year 1980 for the National Aeronautics and Space Administration. | H.R. 1786 | Feb. 1 | ST | CST | Mar. 19 | June 11 | 96-52 | 96-207 | H 1779 | S 7671 | Mar. 28 | June 14 | Aug. 8 | 96-48 |
| Extending, for the academic year 1979-80, certain programs under the Higher Education Act. | H.R. 4476 | June 14 | EdL App | | July 5 July 19 | | 96-318 | | H 6916 | S 11044 | July 31 | July 31 | Aug. 13 | 96-49 |
| Authorizing the President to designate the week of September 16 to 22, 1979, as "National Lupus Week". | H.J. Res. 19 (S.J. Res. 99) | Jan. 15 | POCS | Jud | July 17 | Aug. 1 | 96-340 | | H 6356 | S 11347 | July 20 | Aug. 2 | Aug. 13 | 96-50 |
| Designating the week of October 8 through October 14, 1979, as "National Diabetes Week". | H.J. Res. 209 (S.J. Res. 98) | Feb. 15 | POCS | Jud | July 17 | July 31 | 96-341 | 96-278 | H 6356 | S 11346 | July 20 | Aug. 2 | Aug. 13 | 96-51 |
| To allow the Bureau of the Census a temporary variance in securing space for purposes of taking the 1980 Decennial Census. | S. 1318 | June 12 | | GA | | July 31 | | 96-277 | H 7065 | S 11268 | Aug. 2 | Aug. 1 | Aug. 13 | 96-52 |
| Authorizing funds for fiscal year 1980 for international development and economic assistance programs. | H.R. 3324 (S. 588) | Mar. 29 | FA | FR | Mar. 31 | May 15 | 96-79 | | H 2178 | S 8001 | Apr. 10 | June 19 | Aug. 14 | 95-53 |
| Making certain technical and clerical amendments to title 5, United States Code. | H.R. 4616 | June 26 | | GA | | July 31 | | 96-276 | H 5623 | S 11367 | July 10 | Aug. 2 | Aug. 14 | 96-54 |
| To provide for the relief of the City of Nenana, Alaska.. | H.R. 4811 (S. 1479) | July 16 | IIA | ENR | July 25 | July 18 | 96-387 | 96-250 | H 6834 | S 11179 | July 30 | Aug. 1 | Aug. 14 | 96-55 |
| To provide for repayment of certain student loan debts federally insured or guaranteed which arise in bankruptcy proceedings unless determined otherwise by the courts. | H.R. 2807 | Mar. 13 | | Jud | | June 21 | | 96-230 | H 2758 | S 9160 | May 7 | July 11 | Aug. 14 | 96-56 |
| To increase the amount authorized for the District of Columbia share of the cost of the rapid transit system of the National Capital Region. | H.R. 3914 | May 3 | DC | GA | May 9 | July 27 | 96-132 | 96-263 | H 3654 | S 11344 | May 23 | Aug. 2 | Aug. 14 | 96-57 |
| Authorizing an additional $620 million in supplemental funds for fiscal year 1979 for the Food Stamp Program. | H.R. 4057 (S. 1309) | May 10 | Agr | Agr | June 11 | July 6 | 96-264 | 96-236 | H 5753 | S 10353 | July 11 | July 23 | Aug. 14 | 96-58 |
| Directing the Secretary of Agriculture to convey to Bell County, Kentucky, Board of Education, a reversion interest on land held by the United States. | S. 41 | Jan. 15 | Agr | Agr | June 15 | Mar. 27 | 96-277 | 96-48 | H 6377 | S 3859 | July 23 | Apr. 4 | Aug. 14 | 96-59 |
| Authorizing funds for fiscal years 1980 and 1981 for the Department of State, International Communication Agency, and Board for International Broadcasting, and authorizing supplemental funds for fiscal year 1979 for the Department of State. | H.R. 3363 (S. 586) | Apr. 2 | FA | FR | Apr. 3 | May 3 | 96-81 | 96-116 | H 2293 | S 5913 | Apr. 24 | May 15 | Aug. 15 | 96-60 |
| Authorizing funds for fiscal years 1980, 1981, and 1982, for programs administered by the Fisheries Conservation and Management Act. | S. 917 (H.R. 1798) | Apr. 9 | MMF | CST | May 15 | Apr. 23 | 96-170 | 96-72 | H 5039 | S 4908 | June 25 | Apr. 30 | Aug. 15 | 96-61 |
| To authorize and request the President to issue annually a proclamation designating the first Sunday of September following Labor Day of each year as "National Grandparents Day". | H.J. Res. 244 | Mar. 8 | | | | | | | H 6815 | S 11632 | July 27 | Aug. 3 | Sept. 6 | 96-62 |
| Authorizing funds for fiscal years 1980, 1981 and 1982 for the Safe Drinking Water Act. | S. 1146 (H.R. 3509) | May 15 | IFC | EPW | May 15 | May 15 | 96-186 | 96-161 | H 6846 | S 6302 | July 30 | May 22 | Sept. 6 | 96-63 |
| To extend the time for foreign banks to obtain required deposit insurance with respect to existing branches in the United States. | S. 1646 | Aug. 2 | | BHUA | | Aug. 2 | | 96-301 | H 7456 | S 12036 | Sept. 7 | Sept. 6 | Sept. 14 | 96-64 |
| Authorizing the President to proclaim the week of September 16 through 22, 1979, as "National Meals on | H.J. Res. 367 | June 26 | | Jud | | Sept. 14 | | 96-318 | H 7066 | S 12693 | Aug. 2 | Sept. 14 | Sept. 19 | 96-65 |

| | | | | | | | | | | | | | | | |
|---|---|---|---|---|---|---|---|---|---|---|---|---|---|---|---|
| Authorizing funds for fiscal years 1980 and 1981 for the Arms Control and Disarmament Agency. | H.R. | 2774 | Mar. 8 | FA | FR | Mar. 16 | Apr. 26 | 96–47 | 96–95 | H 1591 | S 5108 | Mar. 22 | May 1 | Sept. 21 | 96–66 |
| To eliminate the present prohibition in the U.S. aid program against any form of assistance being given to Uganda. | S. (H.R. 3897) | 1019 | Apr. 26 | ......... | FR | ......... | May 3 | ......... | ......... | H 3478 | S 5417 | May 21 | May 7 | Sept. 21 | 96–67 |
| Making appropriations for fiscal year 1980 for the Departments of State, Justice, Commerce, the Judiciary and related agencies. | H.R. | 4392 | June 7 | App | App | June 7 | July 19 | 96–247 | 96–251 | H 5843 | S 10438 | July 12 | July 24 | Sept. 24 | 96–68 |
| Making appropriations for fiscal year 1980 for energy and water resources development projects. | H.R. | 4388 | June 7 | App | App | June 7 | July 12 | 96–243 | 96–242 | H 4665 | S 9722 | June 18 | July 18 | Sept. 25 | 96–69 |
| To provide for the operation and maintenance of the Panama Canal, and to provide for the exercise of the rights and performance of the duties of the United States provided in the Panama Canal Treaty of 1977. | H.R. | 111 | Jan. 15 | MMF<br>FA<br>Jud<br>POCS | AS | Apr. 23<br>June 7 | July 21 | 96–98 | 96–255 | H 4901 | S 10648 | June 21 | July 26 | Sept. 27 | 96–70 |
| Extending until November 1, 1979, Federal Housing Administration mortgage insurance authorities. | S.J. Res. | 105 | Sept. 25 | ......... | ......... | ......... | ......... | ......... | ......... | H 8523 | S 13441 | Sept. 26 | Sept. 25 | Sept. 28 | 96–71 |
| To extend the Export Administration Act through fiscal year 1983 and to authorize $8 million for each of fiscal years 1980 and 1981 to provide authority to regulate exports. | S. (H.R. 4034) | 737 | Mar. 22 | FA | BHUA | May 15 | May 15 | 96–200 | 96–169 | H 8473 | S 10203 | Sept. 25 | July 21 | Sept. 29 | 96–72 |
| Authorizing funds for fiscal years 1980 through 1982 for Amtrak. | H.R. (S. 712) | 3996 | May 8 | IFC | CST | May 15 | May 15 | 96–189 | 96–183 | H 6581 | S 11367 | July 25 | Aug. 2 | Sept. 29 | 96–73 |
| Making appropriations for fiscal year 1980 for the Department of the Treasury and the U.S. Postal Service. | H.R. | 4393 | June 7 | App | App | June 7 | Aug. 2 | 96–248 | 96–299 | H 5985 | S 11987 | July 16 | Sept. 6 | Sept. 29 | 96–74 |
| To continue in effect any authority provided under the Department of Justice Authorization Act for fiscal year 1979, for a certain period. | H.R. | 5380 | Sept. 25 | ......... | ......... | ......... | ......... | ......... | ......... | H 8509 | S 13612 | Sept. 26 | Sept. 27 | Sept. 29 | 96–75 |
| Authorizing funds through fiscal year 1980 for nurse training programs. | S. (H.R. 3633) | 230 | Jan. 25 | IFC | LHR | May 15 | Apr. 30 | 96–183 | 96–101 | H 6797 | S 5421 | July 27 | May 7 | Sept. 29 | 96–76 |
| Extending by 120 days the expiration date of the Defense Production Act. | H.J. Res. | 406 | Sept. 21 | ......... | ......... | ......... | ......... | ......... | ......... | H 8442 | S 13612 | Sept. 25 | Sept. 27 | Sept. 29 | 96–77 |
| Providing for a combined permanent and temporary limit on the public debt of $879 billion through May 31, 1980. | H.R. | 5369 | Sept. 21 | WM<br>R | ......... | Sept. 24 | ......... | 96–472 | ......... | H 8527 | S 13651 | Sept. 26 | Sept. 28 | Sept. 29 | 96–78 |
| To revise and extend through fiscal year 1982, programs administered under the Public Health Service Act. | S. (H.R. 3917) | 544 | Mar. 5 | IFC | LHR | May 15 | Apr. 26 | 96–190 | 96–96 | H 6248 | S 5113 | July 19 | May 1 | Oct. 4 | 96–79 |
| Authorizing and requesting the President to issue a proclamation designating the seven calendar days beginning October 7, 1979, as "National Port Week". | H.J. Res. | 303 | Apr. 24 | ......... | Jud | ......... | Oct. 2 | ......... | ......... | H 8238 | S 13907 | Sept. 20 | Oct. 2 | Oct. 6 | 96–80 |
| Authorizing funds for fiscal year 1980 for the United States Commission on Civil Rights. | S. (H.R. 2641) | 721 | Mar. 21 | Jud | Jud | May 1 | May 15 | 96–109 | 96–167 | H 4279 | S 7182 | June 8 | June 7 | Oct. 6 | 96–81 |
| To clarify and expand jurisdiction of U.S. magistrates and improve access to the Federal courts. | S. (H.R. 1046) | 237 | Jan 25 | Jud | Jud | June 20 | Apr. 24 | 96–287 | 96–74 | H 5102 | S 5151 | June 26 | May 2 | Oct. 10 | 96–82 |
| Authorizing funds through fiscal year 1984 for the Office of Federal Procurement Policy. | S. (H.R. 3763) | 756 | Mar. 26 | GO | GA | May 15 | May 15 | 96–178 | 96–144 | H 7605 | S 6251 | Sept. 10 | May 21 | Oct. 10 | 96–83 |
| To extend until July 1, 1980, the final report due date of the National Commission on Unemployment Compensation, and to extend until January 1, 1982, exclusion of certain alien farm workers from the Federal unemployment tax. | H.R. | 3920 | May 3 | WM | Fin | June 5 | Sept. 21 | 96–237 | 96–327 | H 6612 | S 13611 | July 25 | Sept. 27 | Oct. 10 | 96–84 |
| Authorizing funds for the U.S. Travel Service for fiscal year 1980. | S. (H.R. 2797) | 233 | Jan. 25 | WM | CST | June 7 | Mar. 1 | 96–250 | 96–8 | H 8730 | S 2348 | July 16 | Mar. 8 | Oct. 10 | 96–85 |
| Making continuing appropriations through November 20, 1979, for the Federal Government. | H.J. Res. | 412 | Oct. 9 | App | App | Oct. 9 | Oct. 10 | 96–500 | ......... | H 8850 | S 14325 | Oct. 9 | Oct. 10 | Oct. 12 | 96–86 |
| Authorizing the Secretary of the Interior to provide for the commemoration of the efforts of Goodloe Byron in protecting the Appalachian Trail. | H.R. | 5419 | Sept. 27 | ......... | ......... | ......... | ......... | ......... | ......... | H 8592 | S 13781 | Sept. 27 | Oct. 1 | Oct. 12 | 96–87 |
| To establish a Department of Education.............. | S. (H.R. 2444) | 210 | Jan. 24 | GO | GA | May 14 | Mar. 27 | 96–143 | 96–49 | H 5725 | S 4897 | July 11 | Apr. 30 | Oct. 17 | 96–88 |
| Increasing the annual authorization for the Canal Zone Biological Area (the Barro Colorado Island Facility of the Tropical Research Institute of the Smithsonian Institution). | S. | 817 | Mar. 8 | MMF | RAdm | Aug. 2 | May 8 | 96–405 | 96–120 | H 8823 | S 5721 | Oct. 9 | May 14 | Oct. 19 | 96–89 |

| Title | Bill No. | Date introduced | Committee | | Date reported | | Report No. | | Page of passage in Congressional Record | | Date of passage | | Public Law | |
|---|---|---|---|---|---|---|---|---|---|---|---|---|---|---|
| | | | House | Senate | House | Senate | House | Senate | House | Senate | House | Senate | Date approved | No. |
| To permit American manufacturers to ship lottery tickets and related material in connection therewith to foreign countries where lotteries are legal. | H.R. 1301 (S. 947) | Jan. 23 | Jud | Jud | Mar. 15 | Sept. 19 | 96–45 | 96–323 | H 2270 | S 14321 | Apr. 24 | Oct. 10 | Oct. 23 | 96–90 |
| To allow the U.S. Attorney and Assistant U.S. Attorneys for the Eastern District of New York to reside within twenty miles of the district. | S. 567 (H.R. 3959) | Mar. 7 | Jud | Jud | Sept. 28 | Apr. 25 | 96–489 | 96–94 | H 9164 | S 5160 | Oct. 15 | May 2 | Oct. 25 | 96–91 |
| Authorizing funds for fiscal year 1980 for international security assistance programs. | H.R. 3173 (S. 584) | Mar. 22 | FA | FR | Mar. 24 | May 11 May 15 | 96–70 | 96–136 | H 1814 | S 6370 | Mar. 29 | May 22 | Oct. 29 | 96–92 |
| Making appropriations for fiscal year 1980 for the District of Columbia government. | H.R. 4580 | June 21 | App | App | June 21 | July 24 | 96–294 | 96–257 | H 6074 | S 10735 | July 17 | July 27 | Oct. 30 | 96–93 |
| To extend certain authorities relating to the international energy program. | H.R. 5506 | Oct. 9 | IFC | ENR | Oct. 11 | ......... | 96–511 | ......... | H 9477 | S 15486 | Oct. 22 | Oct. 31 | Oct. 31 | 96–94 |
| To protect the archaeological resources of land owned or controlled by the United States. | H.R. 1825 (S. 490) | Feb. 1 | IIA | ENR | June 28 | May 15 | 96–311 | 96–179 | H 5509 | S 10842 | July 9 | July 30 | Oct. 31 | 96–95 |
| To provide that any reduction in the 1980 appropriations for community service and continuing education programs be borne equally by all States. | H.R. 5386 | Sept. 25 | EdL | LHR | Oct. 4 | ......... | 96–497 | ......... | H 9178 | S 14802 | Oct. 15 | Oct. 18 | Oct. 31 | 96–96 |
| To increase the amount of debt which may be incurred by the Tennessee Valley Authority in the financing of its power operations over the next five years. | S. 436 (H.R. 2686) | Feb. 21 | PWT | EPW | Sept. 28 | May 15 | 96–491 | 96–175 | H 9474 | S 8097 | Oct. 22 | June 20 | Oct. 31 | 96–97 |
| Authorizing funds for fiscal years 1980 and 1981 for the National Historical Publications and Records Commission. | H.R. 3923 | May 3 | GO | GA | May 11 | Aug. 1 | 96–141 | 96–283 | H 3479 | S 13307 | May 21 | Sept. 25 | Nov. 1 | 96–98 |
| Designating November 4, 1979, as "Will Rogers Day"... | H.J. Res. 3 (S.J. Res. 32) | Jan. 15 | ......... | ......... | ......... | ......... | ......... | ......... | H 9765 | S 15528 | Oct. 26 | Oct. 31 | Nov. 2 | 96–99 |
| Authorizing funds for fiscal year 1980 for intelligence operations of the Federal Government. | S. 975 (H.R. 3821) | Apr. 23 | Intel AS | Intel AS | May 8 May 15 | Apr. 18 June 11 | 96–127 | 96–71 96–206 | H 5622 | S 8094 | July 10 | June 20 | Nov. 2 | 96–100 |
| To provide for the orderly restructuring of the Milwaukee Railroad. | S. 1905 (H.J.Res. 341) | Oct. 17 | IFC | CST | May 30 | Oct. 29 | 96–225 | ......... | H 9931 | S 15455 | Oct. 30 | Oct. 30 | Nov. 4 | 96–101 |
| To grant authority to the President to create an emergency program to conserve energy. | S. 1030 | Apr. 26 | IFC | ENR | July 23 | May 4 | 96–373 | 96–117 | H 7048 | S 6931 | Aug. 1 | June 5 | Nov. 5 | 96–102 |
| Making appropriations for fiscal year 1980 for the Department of Housing and Urban Development, and for sundry independent agencies, boards, commissions, corporations, and offices. | H.R. 4394 | June 7 | App | App | June 7 | July 24 | 96–249 | 96–258 | H 5212 | S 10759 | June 27 | July 27 | Nov. 5 | 96–103 |
| To provide a temporary exemption from State usury ceilings on certain business and agriculture loans. | H.R. 2515 | Feb. 28 | ......... | BHUA | ......... | Oct. 11 | ......... | 96–364 | H 8344 | S 14479 | Sept. 24 | Oct. 12 | Nov. 5 | 96–104 |
| To provide for a fifteen day temporary extension of certain Federal Housing Administration authorities. | S.J. Res. 117 | Oct. 29 | ......... | ......... | ......... | ......... | ......... | ......... | H 10255 | S 15353 | Nov. 7 | Oct. 29 | Nov. 8 | 96–105 |
| Proposing revisions in the highway safety and public transportation programs. | H.R. 4249 | May 30 | PWT | EPW | June 20 | Sept. 28 | 96–288 | 96–333 | H 5494 | S 14999 | July 9 | Oct. 24 | Nov. 9 | 96–106 |
| Authorizing funds for fiscal year 1980 for military procurement programs of the Department of Defense. | S. 428 (H.R. 4040) | Feb. 9 | AS | AS | May 15 | May 31 | 96–166 | 96–197 | H 7935 | S 7538 | Sept. 14 | June 13 | Nov. 9 | 96–107 |
| Making appropriations for Agriculture, Rural Development, and Related Agencies programs, for fiscal year ending September 30, 1980. | H.R. 4387 | June 7 | App | App | June 7 | July 12 | 96–242 | 96–246 | H 4736 | S 9836 | June 19 | July 19 | Nov. 9 | 96–108 |
| Authorizing $25 million for special Caribbean hurricane relief assistance. | H.R. 5218 | Sept. 7 | ......... | FR | ......... | Oct. 15 | ......... | 96–367 | H 8441 | S 15373 | Sept. 25 | Oct. 30 | Nov. 9 | 96–109 |
| Authorizing additional funds for fiscal years 1980 and 1981 for the Department of State for refugee assistance programs. | H.R. 4955 (S. 1668) | July 25 | FA | FR | July 27 | Oct. 16 | 96–398 | 96–370 | H 9744 | S 15758 | Oct. 25 | Nov. 2 | Nov. 13 | 96–110 |

| Description | Bill No. | | Committee (House) | Committee (Senate) | | | Report | Report | | | | | | Public Law |
|---|---|---|---|---|---|---|---|---|---|---|---|---|---|---|
| To provide for the operation of the S.S. *United States*, the S.S. *Santa Rosa*, and the S.S. *Independence* in domestic and/or foreign commerce of the United States, primarily in cruise trade between the Hawaiian Islands and the Mainland. | S. 1281 | (H.R. 5472) | June 5 | MMF | CST | Oct. 26 | Aug. 2 | 96-559 | 96-298 | H 9905 | S 12036 | Oct. 30 | Sept. 6 | Nov. 15 | 96-111 |
| Authorizing funds for fiscal year 1980 for the Maritime Administration, Department of Commerce. | S. 640 | (H.R. 2462) | Mar. 13 | MMF | CST | May 15 | May 1 | 96-169 | 96-105 | H 6785 | S 6630 | July 27 | May 24 | Nov. 16 | 96-112 |
| To amend the Agricultural Act of 1938, as amended, to exempt State prison farms from paying of marketing quota penalties. | H.R. 998 | (S. 312) | Jan. 18 | Agr | Agr | July 27 | Oct. 29 | 96-393 | 96-380 | H 7953 | S 15695 | Sept. 17 | Nov. 1 | Nov. 16 | 96-113 |
| To establish a Congressional award program for the purpose of recognizing excellence and leadership among young people. | H.R. 2196 | (S. 221) | Feb. 15 | EdL | GA | Oct. 16 | July 12 | 96-518 | 96-245 | H 9837 | S 15692 | Oct. 29 | Nov. 1 | Nov. 16 | 96-114 |
| Authorizing the President to designate the week beginning November 18, 1979, as "National Family Week". | H.J. Res. 68 | (S.J. Res. 41) | Jan. 15 | | Jud | | Aug. 2 | | | H 10441 | S 16490 | Nov. 8 | Nov. 9 | Nov. 16 | 96-115 |
| Providing for the U.S. distribution of the International Communication Agency film entitled "Reflections: George Meany". | H.R. 5279 | | Sept. 13 | | FR | | Oct. 31 | | 96-392 | H 8340 | S 16038 | Sept. 24 | Nov. 6 | Nov. 16 | 96-116 |
| To correct a land description as contained in Public Law 95-498, providing that certain public lands be held by the United States in trust for the Santa Ana Pueblo Indians. | H.J. Res. 199 | | Feb. 8 | IIA | IA | Mar. 27 | Nov. 1 | 96-72 | 96-396 | H 1864 | S 16155 | Apr. 2 | Nov. 7 | Nov. 16 | 96-117 |
| Authorizing funds for fiscal years 1980, 1981, 1982, and 1983, for the Anadromous Fish Conservation Act. | S. 838 | (H.R. 2035) | Mar. 29 | MMF | CST | May 15 | May 15 | 96-173 | 96-174 | H 5042 | S 7542 | June 25 | June 18 | Nov. 16 | 96-118 |
| Designating the month of December 1979, as "National Child Abuse Prevention Month". | H.J. Res. 428 | | Oct. 23 | | | | | | | H 9764 | S 16159 | Oct. 26 | Nov. 7 | Nov. 16 | 96-119 |
| Designating the U.S. Federal Courthouse Building in San Antonio, Texas, as the "John H. Wood, Jr., Federal Courthouse". | S. 1728 | (H.R. 4619) | Sept. 10 | PWT | EPW | Sept. 14 | Oct. 4 | 96-432 | 96-359 | H 9160 | S 14546 | Oct. 15 | Oct. 12 | Nov. 16 | 96-120 |
| Authorizing funds for the U.S. Fire Administration and for the Center for Fire Research. | S. 1160 | (H.R. 4016) | May 16 | ST | CST | May 15 | May 15 | 96-176 | 96-186 | H 4003 | S 6513 | June 4 | May 23 | Nov. 16 | 96-121 |
| To establish the District of Columbia Retirement Board to manage the retirement funds of D.C. firefighters, police officers, teachers, and judges. | S. 1037 | (H.R. 3939) | Apr. 30 | DC | GA | May 15 | July 9 | 96-155 | 96-237 | H 8372 | S 11268 | Sept. 24 | Aug. 1 | Nov. 17 | 96-122 |
| Making continuing appropriations for fiscal year 1980 for the Federal Government. | H.J. Res. 440 | | Nov. 9 | App | App | Nov. 9 | Nov. 14 | 96-609 | | H 10605 | S 16720 | Nov. 13 | Nov. 15 | Nov. 20 | 96-123 |
| To allow the Interest Rate Modification Act of 1979, passed by the Council of the District of Columbia, to take effect immediately. | H.R. 5811 | | Nov. 7 | DC | | Nov. 8 | | 96-603 | | H 10600 | S 16915 | Nov. 13 | Nov. 16 | Nov. 20 | 96-124 |
| Authorizing funds for fiscal year 1980 for military construction programs of the Department of Defense. | S. 1319 | (H.R. 3947) | June 12 | AS | AS<br>LHR | May 15 | June 12<br>July 26 | 96-149 | 96-209<br>96-259 | H 9623 | S 10823 | Oct. 24 | July 30 | Nov. 26 | 96-125 |
| Appropriating funds for fiscal year 1980 for the Department of the Interior and related agencies. | H.R. 4930 | | July 23 | App | App | July 23 | Oct. 10 | 96-374 | 96-363 | H 6888 | S 14783 | July 30 | Oct. 18 | Nov. 27 | 96-126 |
| To extend through September 30, 1981, the current price-support levels for dairy products. | H.R. 4167 | (S. 6) | May 22 | Agr | Agr | June 15 | Nov. 6 | 96-278 | 96-400 | H 10426 | S 16826 | Nov. 8 | Nov. 15 | Nov. 28 | 96-127 |
| To provide for a cost-of-living increase in the rates of service-connected disability compensation for veterans and in dependency and indemnity compensation for surviving spouses and children of veterans that reflects an actual increase in the Consumer Price Index. | H.R. 2282 | (S. 689) | Feb. 21 | VA | VA<br>App | June 27 | July 27<br>July 31 | 96-310 | 96-260<br>96-280 | H 5945 | S 11629 | July 16 | Aug. 3 | Nov. 28 | 96-128 |
| Authorizing funds for fiscal years 1980 and 1981 for the Natural Gas Pipeline Safety Act, to clarify and expand the authority of the Department of Transportation over liquefied natural gas and natural gas transportation safety, and to establish a statutory framework to regulate the transportation of hazardous liquids. | S. 441 | (H.R. 51) | Feb. 9 | IFC<br>PWT | CST | May 15<br>June 22 | May 15 | 96-201 | 96-182 | H 8025 | S 6774 | Sept. 18 | June 4 | Nov. 30 | 96-129 |
| Making appropriations for fiscal year 1980 for military construction programs of the Department of Defense. | H.R. 4391 | | June 7 | App | App | June 7 | Nov. 8 | 96-246 | 96-407 | H 4675 | S 16526 | June 18 | Nov. 13 | Nov. 30 | 96-130 |
| Making appropriations for fiscal year 1980 for the Department of Transportation. | H.R. 4440 | | June 13 | App | App | July 23 | Oct. 25 | 96-272 | | H 8068 | S 15661 | Sept. 18 | Nov. 1 | Nov. 30 | 96-131 |
| Authorizing funds for fiscal year 1980 for the Department of Justice. | S. 1157 | (H.R. 3303) | May 15 | Jud<br>IFC<br>Intel | Jud | Apr. 23<br>May 8<br>May 15 | May 15 | 96-99 | 96-173 | H 9222 | S 6811 | Oct. 16 | June 4 | Nov. 30 | 96-132 |

| Title | Bill No. | Date intro-duced | Committee | | Date reported | | Report No. | | Page of passage in Congressional Record | | Date of passage | | Public Law | |
|---|---|---|---|---|---|---|---|---|---|---|---|---|---|---|
| | | | House | Senate | House | Senate | House | Senate | House | Senate | House | Senate | Date ap-proved | No. |
| To extend until June 30, 1980, the existing antitrust exemption for oil companies that participate in the agreement on an international energy program. | S. 1871 (H.R. 4445) | Oct. 10 | IFC | ENR | Oct. 11 | Oct. 16 | 96–510 | ……… | H 9476 | S 14723 | Oct. 22 | Oct. 17 | Nov. 30 | 96–133 |
| Designating the Federal Building in Wilmington, Delaware, as the "J. Caleb Boggs Building". | S. 1686 (H.R. 5228) | Aug. 3 | PWT | EPW | Oct. 18 | Oct. 31 | 96–522 | 96–391 | H 11156 | S 15694 | Nov. 27 | Nov. 1 | Dec. 5 | 96–134 |
| To amend Civil Service retirement provisions as they apply to certain employees of the Bureau of Indian Affairs and of the Indian Health Service who are not entitled to Indian employment preference. | H.R. 1885 | Feb. 5 | POCS IIA App | ……… | July 20 Sept. 11 | ……… | 96–370 | | H 9793 | S 17257 | Oct. 26 | Nov. 26 | Dec. 5 | 96–135 |
| Proclaiming the week of December 3 through December 9, 1979, as "Scouting Recognition Week". | H.J. Res. 448 (S.J. Res. 122) | Nov. 20 | ……… | Jud | ……… | Dec. 4 | ……… | | H 11323 | S 17759 | Nov. 29 | Dec. 4 | Dec. 7 | 96–136 |
| Authorizing funds for fiscal year 1980 for conservation, exploration, development and use of naval petroleum reserves and naval oil shale reserves. | H.R. 3354 | Mar. 29 | AS | AS | Apr. 9 | Sept. 19 | 96–91 | 96–325 | H 2339 | S 13611 | Apr. 25 | Sept. 27 | Dec. 12 | 96–137 |
| Authorizing the President to present a gold medal to the American Red Cross. | H.R. 4259 | May 31 | ……… | BHUA | ……… | Nov. 28 | ……… | 96–429 | H 9165 | S 17758 | Oct. 15 | Dec. 4 | Dec. 12 | 96–138 |
| Designating the Federal building at 211 Main Street, in Scott City, Kansas, as the "Henry D. Parkinson Federal Building". | S. 1491 (H.R. 4532) | July 12 | PWT | EPW | Nov. 27 | Oct. 31 | 96–663 | 96–389 | H 11412 | S 15692 | Dec. 3 | Nov. 1 | Dec. 12 | 96–139 |
| Naming a certain Federal building in Rochester, New York, the "Kenneth B. Keating Building". | S. 1535 (H.R. 4845) | July 18 | PWT | EPW | Nov. 27 | Oct. 31 | 96–664 | 96–389 | H 11413 | S 15693 | Dec. 3 | Nov. 1 | Dec. 12 | 96–140 |
| Designating the Department of Labor Building in Washington, D.C., as the "Frances Perkins Department of Labor Building". | S. 1655 (H.R. 5781) | Aug. 2 | PWT | EPW | Nov. 27 | Oct. 31 | 96–665 | 96–388 | H 11414 | S 15692 | Dec. 3 | Nov. 1 | Dec. 12 | 96–141 |
| Authorizing funds for programs relating to emergency medical services systems. | S. 497 (H.R. 3642) | Feb. 26 | IFC | LHR | May 15 | Apr. 30 | 96–185 | 96–102 | H 8734 | S 5525 | Sept. 28 | May 9 | Dec. 12 | 96–142 |
| Authorizing funds for programs under the Domestic Volunteer Service Act of 1973. | S. 239 (H.R. 2859) | Jan. 25 | EdL | LHR | May 15 | Apr. 26 | 96–164 | 96–99 | H 8894 | S 8136 | Oct. 10 | June 20 | Dec. 13 | 96–143 |
| Authorizing the apportionment to the States funds for for Interstate Highway System for fiscal year 1980. | H.R. 5871 | Nov. 13 | PWT | ……… | Nov. 14 | ……… | 96–620 | ……… | H 10799 | S 17540 | Nov. 15 | Nov. 29 | Dec. 13 | 96–144 |
| Waiving the time limitations on the period within which certain military decorations can be awarded to members of the unit involved in the Battle of the Bulge. | H.R. 3407 | Apr. 3 | AS | AS | Sept. 24 | Nov. 20 | 96–470 | 96–422 | H 9103 | S 17623 | Oct. 15 | Nov. 30 | Dec. 14 | 96–145 |
| To fix the annual rates of pay for the Architect of the Capitol and the Assistant Architect of the Capitol. | H.R. 4732 | July 10 | POCS | ……… | July 17 | ……… | 96–349 | ……… | H 7634 | S 17688 | Sept. 10 | Dec. 3 | Dec. 14 | 96–146 |
| Authorizing the President to designate December 18 as "National Unity Day". | H.J. Res. 458 | Dec. 5 | ……… | ……… | ……… | ……… | ……… | | H 11813 | S 18472 | Dec. 11 | Dec. 13 | Dec. 16 | 96–147 |
| To repeal the industrial cost recovery provision of the Clean Water Act. | S. 901 (H.R. 4023) | Apr. 5 | PWT | EPW | June 25 | June 5 | 96–305 | 96–200 | H 5101 | S 7654 | June 14 | June 26 | Dec. 16 | 96.148 |
| To provide for a small business representative as a permanent member of the National Consumer Cooperative Bank Board of Directors. | S. 1788 | Sept. 21 | ……… | BHUA | ……… | Sept. 21 | ……… | 96–328 | H 11583 | S 13611 | Dec. 5 | Sept. 27 | Dec. 16 | 96–149 |
| Authorizing the sale of certain excess U.S. naval vessels to certain foreign nations. | H.R. 5163 | Sept. 5 | AS | AS | Sept. 19 | Nov. 19 | 96–445 | 96–420 | H 8336 | S 18006 | Sept. 25 | Dec. 6 | Dec. 20 | 96–150 |
| To review and extend through fiscal year 1982 programs of grants to State homes for veterans and the exchange of medical information. | H.R. 3892 (S. 1039) | May 2 | VA | VA | May 10 | May 15 | 96–138 | 96–177 | H 3471 | S 7846 | May 21 | June 18 | Dec. 20 | 96–151 |
| Establishing the position of Chief of the Capitol Police Force as a Congressional office. | H.R. 5651 | Oct. 19 | HA | RAdm | Nov. 1 | Nov. 30 | 96–581 | 96–436 | H 10414 | S 18009 | Nov. 8 | Dec. 6 | Dec. 20 | 96–152 |
| To amend and extend certain Federal laws relating to housing, community and neighborhood development and preservation, and related programs. | H.R. 3875 (S. 903) (S. 1064) (S. 1149) | May 2 | BFUH | BHUA | May 15 | May 15 | 96–154 | 96–145 96–157 96–164 | H 4214 | S 9399 | June 7 | July 13 | Dec. 21 | 96–153 |
| Making appropriations for the Department of Defense for the fiscal year ending September 30, 1980. | H.R. 5359 | Sept. 20 | App | App | Sept. 20 | Nov. 1 | 96–450 | 96–393 | H 8713 | S 16415 | Sept. 28 | Nov. 9 | Dec. 21 | 96–154 |

| Subject | Bill | No. | Introduced | | | | | Rept. No. | | | | | | Approved | Public Law |
|---|---|---|---|---|---|---|---|---|---|---|---|---|---|---|---|
| Act, as amended, with respect to the Government contribution toward subscription charge. | S. | 710 | Mar. 21 | POCS | GA | | May 15 | | 96-154 | H 12128 | S 6375 | Dec. 17 | May 22 | Dec. 27 | 96-156 |
| To restructure the Federal Law Enforcement Assistance Administration, to assist State and local governments in improving the quality of their justice systems. | S. (H.R. 2061) | 241 | Jan. 29 | Jud | Jud | May 15 | May 14 | 96-163 | 96-142 | H 9114 | S 6230 | Oct. 12 | May 21 | Dec. 27 | 96-157 |
| To grant to the Little Sisters of the Poor all right, title, and interest of the United States in the land comprising certain alleys in the District of Columbia. | H.R. | 5645 | Oct. 18 | DC | | Oct. 24 | | 96-551 | | H 11177 | S 19100 | Nov. 27 | Dec. 18 | Dec. 27 | 96-158 |
| To authorize appropriations to carry out the Endangered Species Act of 1973 during fiscal years 1980, 1981, and 1982. | S. (H.R. 2218) | 1143 | May 15 | MMF | EPW | May 15 | May 15 | 96-167 | 96-151 | H 9656 | S 7557 | Oct. 24 | June 13 | Dec. 28 | 96-159 |
| To amend the District of Columbia Self-Government and Governmental Reorganization Act with respect to the borrowing authority of the District of Columbia. | H.R. | 5537 | Oct. 11 | DC | GA | Oct. 24 | Dec. 13 | 96-550 | 96-487 | H 11175 | S 19374 | Nov. 27 | Dec. 20 | Dec. 28 | 96-160 |
| To authorize transfer accounts at commercial banks, remote service units at Federal savings and loan associations, and share draft accounts at Federal credit unions during the period beginning on December 31, 1979, and ending on April 1, 1980. | H.R. | 4998 | July 27 | BFUA | BHUA | Sept. 7 | Nov. 20 | 96-421 | 96-423 | H 7962 | S 18151 | Sept. 17 | Dec. 10 | Dec. 28 | 96-161 |
| To authorize the Secretary of the Interior to engage in a feasibility study. | S. (H.R. 2757) | 585 | Mar. 8 | IIA | ENR | | July 16 | | 96-248 | H 11689 | S 10407 | Dec. 10 | July 23 | Dec. 28 | 96-162 |
| Granting the consent of Congress to the compact between the States of New York and New Jersey providing for the coordination, facilitation, promotion, preservation, and protection of trade and commerce in and through the Port of New York District through the financing and effectuation of industrial development projects. | H.R. | 4943 | July 24 | Jud | Jud | Oct. 10 | Nov. 27 | 96-507 | 96-427 | H 9506 | S 18007 | Oct. 23 | Dec. 6 | Dec. 28 | 96-163 |
| To authorize appropriations for the Department of Energy for national security programs for fiscal year 1980. | S. (H.R. 2603) | 673 | Mar. 15 | AS | AS ENR | May 15 | May 22 | 96-162 | 96-193 | H 10493 | S 7843 | Nov. 9 | June 18 | Dec. 29 | 96-164 |
| To incorporate United Service Organizations, Incorporated. | H.R. (S. 2113) | 600 | Jan. 15 | Jud | Jud | Oct. 10 | Dec. 20 | 96-505 | 96-545 | H 9161 | S 19346 | Oct. 15 | Dec. 20 | Dec. 29 | 96-165 |
| To extend the Federal Physicians Comparability Allowance Act of 1978. | H.R. | 5015 | July 30 | POCS | | Dec. 4 | | 96-683 | | H 11694 | S 19373 | Dec. 10 | Dec. 20 | Dec. 29 | 96-166 |
| To continue through May 31, 1981, the existing prohibition on the issuance of fringe benefit regulations. | H.R. | 5224 | Sept. 10 | WM | Fin | Sept. 20 | Nov. 29 | 96-448 | 96-433 | H 8833 | S 18097 | Oct. 9 | Dec. 7 | Dec. 29 | 96-167 |
| Expressing the sense of Congress concerning the White House Preservation Fund. | H.J. Res. | 462 | Dec. 10 | | | | | | | H 12385 | S 19386 | Dec. 20 | Dec. 20 | Dec. 29 | 96-168 |
| To provide for participation of the United States in the International Energy Exposition. | H.R. (S. 1012) | 5079 | Aug. 2 | | FR | | Oct. 16 | | 96-369 | H 8825 | S 16677 | Oct. 9 | Nov. 14 | Dec. 29 | 96-169 |
| To permit civil suits under section 1979 of the Revised Statutes (42 U.S.C. 1983) against any person acting under color of any law or custom of the District of Columbia who subjects any person within the jurisdiction of the District of Columbia to the deprivation of any right, privilege, or immunity secured by the Constitution and laws. | H.R. | 3343 | Mar. 29 | DC | | | Oct. 20 | | 96-548 | H 11177 | S 19100 | Nov. 27 | Dec. 18 | Dec. 29 | 96-170 |
| To require a study of the desirability of mandatory age retirement for certain pilots. | H.R. | 3948 | May 4 | PWT | CST | Sept. 25 | | 96-474 | | H 11565 | S 18977 | Dec. 5 | Dec. 18 | Dec. 29 | 96-171 |
| To change the name of the Palmetto Bend Reservoir on the Navidad River in Texas to Lake Texana. | H.R. | 2771 | Mar. 8 | IIA | ENR | May 14 | Dec. 12 | 96-142 | 96-482 | H 3452 | S 19373 | May 21 | Dec. 20 | Dec. 29 | 96-172 |
| To provide that any person eligible for medical care under the Civilian Health and Medical Program of the Uniformed Services (CHAMPUS) who is a veteran with a service-connected disability may not be denied care and treatment for such disability under CHAMPUS solely because such person is eligible for care and treatment for such disability in Veterans' Administration facilities. | H.R. | 5025 | July 31 | AS | AS | Sept. 24 | | 96-469 | | H 9164 | S 19369 | Oct. 15 | Dec. 20 | Dec. 29 | 96-173 |
| To amend sec. 209 of title 18, United States Code. | H.R. | 5174 | Sept. 5 | Jud | | Nov. 29 | | 96-674 | | H 12104 | S 19430 | Dec. 17 | Dec. 20 | Dec. 29 | 96-174 |
| To authorize certain transactions involving the acquisition and disposal of strategic and critical materials for the National Defense Stockpile. | H.R. | 595 | Jan. 15 | AS | AS | Mar. 20 | Oct. 3 | 96-56 | 96-338 | H 1896 | S 14651 | Apr. 3 | Oct. 16 | Dec. 29 | 96-175 |

| Title | Bill No. | Date introduced | Committee | | Date reported | | Report No. | | Page of passage in Congressional Record | | Date of passage | | Public Law | |
|---|---|---|---|---|---|---|---|---|---|---|---|---|---|---|
| | | | House | Senate | House | Senate | House | Senate | House | Senate | House | Senate | Date approved | No. |
| To establish an improved program for extra long staple cotton. | H.R. 5523 (S. 1978) | Oct. 10 | Agr | Agr | Dec. 5 | Dec. 4 | 96–688 | 96–445 | H 12130 | S 19274 | Dec. 17 | Dec. 19 | Dec. 31 | 96–176 |
| To modify the method of establishing quotas on the importation of certain meat, to include within such quotas certain meat products. | H.R. 2727 | Mar. 8 | WM | Fin | June 6 | Dec. 7 | 96–238 | 96–465 | H 10661 | S 18968 | Nov. 14 | Dec. 18 | Dec. 31 | 96–177 |
| To extend for 1 year the provisions of law relating to the business expenses of State legislators. | H.R. 3091 | Mar. 19 | WM | ......... | Mar. 21 | ......... | 96–63 | ......... | H 1691 | S 3580 | Mar. 27 | Mar. 28 | Jan. 2 1980 | 96–178 |
| Relating to survivor benefits for certain dependent children. | H.R. 2584 | Mar. 1 | POCS | GA | Oct. 5 | Dec. 14 | 96–499 | 96–503 | H 9479 | S 19293 | Oct. 22 | Dec. 20 | Jan. 2 1980 | 96–179 |
| To revise and extend the Comprehensive Alcohol Abuse and Alcoholism Prevention, Treatment, and Rehabilitation Act of 1970. | S. 440 (H.R. 3916) | Feb. 21 | IFC | LHR | May 15 | Apr. 30 | 96–193 | 96–103 | H 9234 | S 5392 | Oct. 16 | May 7 | Jan. 2 1980 | 96–180 |
| To amend the Drug Abuse Office and Treatment Act of 1972. | S. 525 (H.R. 3916) | Mar. 1 | IFC | LHR | May 15 | Apr. 30 | 96–193 | 96–104 | H 9235 | S 5428 | Oct. 16 | May 7 | Jan. 2 1980 | 96–181 |
| To amend the Water Bank Act for the purposes of authorizing the Secretary of Agriculture to adjust payment rates with respect to initial conservation agreements and to designate certain areas as wetlands. | H.R. 2043 (S. 837) | Feb. 8 | MMF | Agr | May 15 | Dec. 5 | 96–171 | 96–449 | H 5500 | S 18966 | July 9 | Dec. 18 | Jan. 2 1980 | 96–182 |
| Making an urgent appropriation for administrative expenses of the Chrysler Corporation loan guarantee program, and to provide financial assistance to the Chrysler Corporation for the fiscal year ending September 30, 1980. | H.J. Res. 467 | Dec. 19 | App | ......... | Dec. 20 | ......... | 96–719 | ......... | H 12380 | S 19415 | Dec. 20 | Dec. 20 | Jan. 2 1980 | 96–183 |
| To amend the National Capital Transportation Act of 1969 to authorize additional Federal contributions for the cost of construction of the rapid transit system of the National Capital Region, to provide an orderly method for the retirement of bonds issued by the Washington Metropolitan Area Transit Authority. | H.R. 3951 | May 4 | DC | GA | May 15 | Dec. 11 | 96–156 | 96–475 | H 5947 | S 19329 | July 16 | Dec. 20 | Jan. 3 1980 | 96–184 |
| To authorize loan guarantees to the Chrysler Corporation. | H.R. 5860 (S. 2094) | Nov. 9 | BFUA | BHUA | Dec. 6 | Dec. 6 | 96–690 | 96–643 | H 12223 | S 19216 | Dec. 18 | Dec. 19 | Jan. 7 1980 | 96–185 |
| Extending the dates for submission of the President's Budget and Economic Report. | H.J. Res. 468 | Nov. 20 | ......... | ......... | ......... | ......... | ......... | ......... | H 12480 | S 19430 | Dec. 20 | Dec. 20 | Jan. 8 1980 | 96–186 |
| To amend the Federal Election Campaign Act of 1971 to make certain changes in the reporting and disclosure requirements of such Act. | H.R. 5010 (S. 1757) | July 30 | HA | RAdm | Sept. 7 | Sept. 17 | 96–422 | 96–319 | H 7618 | S 19100 | Sept. 10 | Dec. 18 | Jan. 8 1980 | 96–187 |

## TABLE OF COMMITTEE ABBREVIATIONS

| | | | | | |
|---|---|---|---|---|---|
| Aer | Aeronautical and Space Sciences | DC | District of Columbia | HA | House Administration |
| Agr | Agriculture | EdL | Education and Labor | IA | Select Committee on Indian Affairs |
| | Agriculture, Nutrition, and Forestry | Energy | Ad Hoc Committee on Energy | IFC | Interstate and Foreign Commerce |
| App | Appropriations | ENR | Energy and Natural Resources | IIA | Interior and Insular Affairs |
| AS | Armed Services | EPW | Environment and Public Works | Intel | Intelligence |
| BFUA | Banking, Finance and Urban Affairs | FA | Foreign Affairs | Jud | Judiciary |
| BHUA | Banking, Housing and Urban Affairs | Fin | Finance | LHR | Labor and Human Resources |
| BUD | Budget | FR | Foreign Relations | LPW | Labor and Public Welfare |
| CST | Commerce, Science and Transportation | GA | Governmental Affairs | MMF | Merchant Marine and Fisheries |
| | | GO | Government Operations | | |

| | |
|---|---|
| OCS | Outer Continental Shelf |
| POCS | Post Office and Civil Service |
| PW | Public Works |
| PWT | Public Works and Transportation |
| R | Rules |
| RAdm | Rules and Administration |
| SB | Small Business |
| ST | Science and Technology |
| VA | Veterans' Affairs |
| WM | Ways and Means |

# Appendix B

## Bills and Corresponding Public Law Numbers

| | Law No. | | Law No. | | Law No. | | Law No. | | Law No. |
|---|---|---|---|---|---|---|---|---|---|
| S. 7 | 96– 22 | S. 975 | 96–100 | H.R. 1786 | 96– 48 | H.R. 3920 | 96– 84 | H.R. 5224 | 96–167 |
| S. 37 | 96– 3 | S. 976 | 96– 47 | H.R. 1787 | 96– 16 | H.R. 3923 | 96– 98 | H.R. 5279 | 96–116 |
| S. 41 | 96– 59 | S. 984 | 96– 31 | H.R. 1825 | 96– 95 | H.R. 3948 | 96–171 | H.R. 5359 | 96–154 |
| S. 199 | 96– 25 | S. 1007 | 96– 35 | H.R. 1885 | 96–135 | H.R. 3951 | 96–184 | H.R. 5369 | 96– 78 |
| S. 210 | 96– 88 | S. 1019 | 96– 67 | H.R. 1902 | 96– 2 | H.R. 3978 | 96– 37 | H.R. 5380 | 96– 75 |
| S. 230 | 96– 76 | S. 1030 | 96–102 | H.R. 2043 | 96–182 | H.R. 3996 | 96– 73 | H.R. 5386 | 96– 96 |
| S. 233 | 96– 85 | S. 1037 | 96–122 | H.R. 2154 | 96– 41 | H.R. 4057 | 96– 58 | H.R. 5419 | 96– 87 |
| S. 237 | 96– 82 | S. 1143 | 96–159 | H.R. 2196 | 96–114 | H.R. 4167 | 96–127 | H.R. 5506 | 96– 94 |
| S. 239 | 96–143 | S. 1146 | 96– 63 | H.R. 2282 | 96–128 | H.R. 4249 | 96–106 | H.R. 5523 | 96–176 |
| S. 241 | 96–157 | S. 1157 | 96–132 | H.R. 2283 | 96– 10 | H.R. 4259 | 96–138 | H.R. 5537 | 96–160 |
| S. 348 | 96– 20 | S. 1160 | 96–121 | H.R. 2301 | 96– 4 | H.R. 4289 | 96– 38 | H.R. 5645 | 96–158 |
| S. 411 | 96–129 | S. 1281 | 96–111 | H.R. 2439 | 96– 7 | H.R. 4387 | 96–108 | H.R. 5651 | 96–152 |
| S. 428 | 96–107 | S. 1317 | 96– 30 | H.R. 2479 | 96– 8 | H.R. 4388 | 96– 69 | H.R. 5811 | 96–124 |
| S. 429 | 96– 29 | S. 1318 | 96– 52 | H.R. 2515 | 96–104 | H.R. 4391 | 96–130 | H.R. 5860 | 96–185 |
| S. 436 | 96– 97 | S. 1319 | 96–125 | H.R. 2520 | 96– 17 | H.R. 4392 | 96– 68 | H.R. 5871 | 96–144 |
| S. 440 | 96–180 | S. 1491 | 96–139 | H.R. 2534 | 96– 5 | H.R. 4393 | 96– 74 | | |
| S. 497 | 96–142 | S. 1535 | 96–140 | H.R. 2584 | 96–179 | H.R. 4394 | 96–103 | H.J. Res. 1 | 96– 1 |
| S. 525 | 96–181 | S. 1646 | 96– 64 | H.R. 2727 | 96–177 | H.R. 4440 | 96–131 | H.J. Res. 3 | 96– 99 |
| S. 532 | 96– 14 | S. 1655 | 96–141 | H.R. 2729 | 96– 44 | H.R. 4476 | 96– 49 | H.J. Res. 19 | 96– 50 |
| S. 544 | 96– 79 | S. 1686 | 96–134 | H.R. 2771 | 96–172 | H.R. 4537 | 96– 39 | H.J. Res. 68 | 96–115 |
| S. 567 | 96– 91 | S. 1728 | 96–120 | H.R. 2774 | 96– 66 | H.R. 4556 | 96– 33 | H.J. Res. 199 | 96–117 |
| S. 585 | 96–162 | S. 1788 | 96–149 | H.R. 2805 | 96– 19 | H.R. 4580 | 96– 93 | H.J. Res. 209 | 96– 51 |
| S. 613 | 96– 21 | S. 1871 | 96–133 | H.R. 2807 | 96– 56 | H.R. 4591 | 96– 46 | H.J. Res. 244 | 96– 62 |
| S. 631 | 96– 15 | S. 1874 | 96–155 | H.R. 3091 | 96–178 | H.R. 4616 | 96– 54 | H.J. Res. 262 | 96– 11 |
| S. 640 | 96–112 | S. 1905 | 96–101 | H.R. 3173 | 96– 92 | H.R. 4712 | 96– 42 | H.J. Res. 283 | 96– 9 |
| S. 673 | 96–164 | | | H.R. 3324 | 96– 53 | H.R. 4732 | 96–146 | H.J. Res. 303 | 96– 80 |
| S. 709 | 96– 23 | S.J. Res. 14 | 96– 32 | H.R. 3343 | 96–170 | H.R. 4811 | 96– 55 | H.J. Res. 353 | 96– 34 |
| S. 716 | 96–156 | S.J. Res. 71 | 96– 13 | H.R. 3354 | 96–137 | H.R. 4930 | 96–126 | H.J. Res. 367 | 96– 65 |
| S. 721 | 96– 81 | S.J. Res. 80 | 96– 12 | H.R. 3363 | 96– 60 | H.R. 4943 | 96–163 | H.J. Res. 373 | 96– 45 |
| S. 737 | 96– 72 | S.J. Res. 105 | 96– 71 | H.R. 3404 | 96– 18 | H.R. 4955 | 96–110 | H.J. Res. 406 | 96– 77 |
| S. 756 | 96– 83 | S.J. Res. 117 | 96–105 | H.R. 3407 | 96–145 | H.R. 4998 | 96–161 | H.J. Res. 412 | 96– 86 |
| S. 817 | 96– 89 | | | H.R. 3577 | 96– 26 | H.R. 5010 | 96–187 | H.J. Res. 428 | 96–119 |
| S. 838 | 96–118 | H.R. 111 | 96– 70 | H.R. 3661 | 96– 40 | H.R. 5015 | 96–166 | H.J. Res. 440 | 96–123 |
| S. 869 | 96– 28 | H.R. 595 | 96–175 | H.R. 3875 | 96–153 | H.R. 5025 | 96–173 | H.J. Res. 448 | 96–136 |
| S. 901 | 96–148 | H.R. 600 | 96–165 | H.R. 3879 | 96– 27 | H.R. 5079 | 96–169 | H.J. Res. 458 | 96–147 |
| S. 917 | 96– 61 | H.R. 998 | 96–113 | H.R. 3892 | 96–151 | H.R. 5163 | 96–150 | H.J. Res. 462 | 96–168 |
| S. 927 | 96– 36 | H.R. 1147 | 96– 6 | H.R. 3914 | 96– 57 | H.R. 5174 | 96–174 | H.J. Res. 467 | 96–183 |
| S. 961 | 96– 43 | H.R. 1301 | 96– 90 | H.R. 3915 | 96– 24 | H.R. 5218 | 96–109 | H.J. Res. 468 | 96–186 |

**BILL VETOED**

S. 2096—Scientific Study of Dioxins Program

Source: *Congressional Record,* January 3, 1980, p. D1758.

American Enterprise Institute for Public Policy Research
1150 Seventeenth Street, N.W.   Washington, D.C. 20036   (202) 862-5800